21ST CENTURY NETWORKING

21ST CENTURY NETWORKING

HOW TO BECOME A NATURAL NETWORKER

DAVID SOLE AND BELINDA ROBERTS

First published 2015 by
Elliott and Thompson Limited
27 John Street
London WC1N 2BX
www.eandtbooks.com

ISBN: 978-1-78396-231-0

9 8 7 6 5 4 3 2 1

A CIP catalogue record for this book is available from the British Library.

Typeset by Marie Doherty
Printed in the UK by TJ International

Contents

Introduction

Everyone has networks. Whether they are the group of friends that you socialise with, the colleagues that you work with, the people at the sports club that you spend your time with at weekends or the parents of your children's friends, we all have networks. We have been forming them from an early age – the friends we make at school, at university or college and then as we begin our working lives. We rely on relationships for support and help, to enable us to get things done and because, fundamentally, we like being part of a group – indeed, we have a need to be part of a pack, to be 'in the gang' or to belong. It is a basic emotional need.

And so we cultivate our networks – we identify people that we get on with, that we relate to, that we have something in common with and our networks grow and develop. Yet for the most part, we do it intuitively and without thinking about it. When our partners suggest that we have friends round to dinner, we think about the mix of people that we are going to invite. From our list of friends, we consider who will get on with whom, whether the conversation around the dinner table will be enjoyable, humorous and stimulating, perhaps even connecting possible future partners on a 'blind date', and then we try to put together a guest list that meets those needs. We are networking.

When we talk about networking in business, however, most people either admit that they're reluctant to engage with it, or they see it as an 'optional extra' – another task that has to fit into an already crammed diary. And because it is thought to be additional, it is ignored, because, of course, we can all think of something more important that we have to do. Even when people try to connect with us, if we cannot see the immediate value in making a new connection, it is often the first thing to be dropped from the diary. However, unless we invest time in networking, we are limiting our ability to achieve our full potential and the potential to grow and develop our businesses. The sad reality is that most people fail to appreciate the power of a strong network – they don't realise that they need a network until they need it and by that time, it may feel like it's too late. The good news is, it's *never* too late to start networking.

Modern organisations increasingly rely on matrix-based structures – where relationships have to be developed outside of your immediate colleagues and supervisors, and where influence is the way to get things done because you don't have any direct control. Those who do not invest time in developing a strong network are likely to fail, and those who do it well usually succeed.

There's nothing new about networking. In his book *The Tipping Point*, Malcolm Gladwell tells the story of Paul Revere's midnight ride on 18 April 1775 to mobilise the militia as the English forces advanced on Lexington. Revere's social network was so well developed that those within it also took to their horses and, before long, a significant number of militia had been alerted. It was a classic case of Revere making his network really work for him. Revere wasn't the only rider sent out to raise the alarm – a second person, by the name of William Dawes, also set off, heading south, while Revere went north.

Dawes was able to alert a few people, but he did not have the same well-cultivated social network as Revere had, so Dawes failed by comparison. Revere was a social network broker.

In our modern, fast-paced world, people now often change job more frequently than in the past, and when you decide it is time to move onto a new role or challenge, life can prove to be very tough indeed unless you have a well-developed network. Around two thirds of people find their next job through their network, rather than through other channels. So you need a good network of people who know you and your capabilities and, when making your next move, you should focus your time on talking to them, rather than simply sending your CV to recruitment agencies; or update your profile on social media saying 'looking for a new opportunity' – technology and the internet offer many ways of connecting people, so it's important to take advantage of them.

Good networking isn't a random activity. It isn't about accumulating business cards or having hundreds or even thousands of connections on LinkedIn. Networking is for everyone; it's important in your current role as well as for your career development. Why wouldn't you want to do it, and do it well? There is no downside to effective networking.

Nonetheless, you need to have a plan. Decide what you want to achieve next. Then you need to understand how you are going to make the right connections to reach that objective, and from there you have to put your plan into practice. You also need to know the unwritten rules of networking – the informal 'dos and don'ts' and the social graces that go alongside them. As with many things in life, do it badly and it can be incredibly damaging, but do it well and it's wonderfully rewarding. As with any investment, whether of time or money, the payback isn't always immediate, nor sometimes obvious but, rest assured, investing your time in networking does pay off.

So the purpose of this book is threefold:

- We will help you build networks that are powerful and relevant.

- We will teach you the skills of accomplished networking, help you understand how best to build great relationships with differing personalities, and how to keep those relationships alive and flourishing.

- Finally, we will encourage you to make networking part of your daily routine so that, instead of seeing it as a chore, it just becomes part of your daily life, to the point where you don't even have to think about it.

We hope to help you develop yourself professionally and personally. We will endeavour to support you and your networks; our aim is for networking to become part of your daily life. It may be already – you just don't know it. Good luck!

Networking:
What's the Point?

KEY POINTS

▶ Be clear about the purpose of developing your network.

▶ Be specific about who you are targeting and their relevance to you.

▶ Divide your network into three sections: Personal, Internal and External.

In the modern world, where time is at a premium as never before, who wants to spare a thought for anything that doesn't deliver an immediate return or tangible result? Why would you give up time that could be spent with your family, friends, on a hobby or on meeting a work deadline to socialise with someone you don't know that well, might not have met before or who perhaps has nothing to do with your business? It's a waste of time. Isn't it? But networking is a fundamental part of our lives, even if we're unaware of it; it is something we do on a daily basis, in almost every meaningful interaction we have.

As humans, we have some fundamental emotional needs, which have evolved over millions of years:

- The need to belong
- The need to be safe
- The need to be valued
- The need to feel in control

Our networks play to all of these needs – we choose to spend time with the people we relate to the most: we like to feel supported by our mates and colleagues, we enjoy the sense of belonging to a 'tribe', such as the organisation where we work, and we take pleasure from being appreciated. Without this reassurance we feel insecure and anxious, and our self-confidence suffers.

From our earliest days we choose to belong to certain groups of friends, and that continues throughout our lives, although our social groups may have a different purpose and emphasis beyond simply friendship: at university, for example, as well as our friends and the people with whom we share common interests, we find groups that can help us achieve in our studies through peer review, challenge and support, groups that inspire ideas and that support each other. There may be other groups that we associate with – sports teams, drama groups or musical groups – the list is endless. We develop multiple networks without thinking about it and these networks serve us well. And as we get older, they become even more important, supporting our career progression.

So why, when we enter the world of work, do we turn our nose up when people talk about the importance of networking?

One reason relates to the time pressure that we come under when we are in work. Networking is perceived as being 'nice to have' or 'fine to do if you have the time in your diary to do it', but it is often seen as being low priority by many executives and business leaders. A second reason is that networking is often thought to be about attending business events – a cocktail party or a seminar where the purpose is to exchange business cards or increase the number of LinkedIn contacts that you have. These events fill most of us with dread as it means giving up precious leisure time to engage in small talk and socialise with strangers or vague acquaintances. For people who lack self-confidence, such occasions can feel close to purgatory, and they attend them only because they think they have to show their faces, suppressing the fear of rejection and awkward conversations out of a sense of duty, rather than a real desire to achieve something meaningful from the event.

Networking isn't about this. Of course networking events are important, but they are simply a mechanism to serve a greater purpose. The problem is that most people don't know what that purpose is, so they struggle in these environments and therefore don't get the best from them.

Building strong networks is ever more important in our world today, and the ways and means to do it are changing dramatically. Yet the fundamental issue remains – networking needs to be done with purpose. That purpose may vary depending on where you are in terms of your career and family life, but the crux of it is the intention of developing relationships that are mutually beneficial to both parties. Let's consider the following situation:

CASE STUDY

John was a successful partner with an international accountancy firm and he had just moved from the UK to Hong Kong with his wife Anna and their two young children. As a single man, he had undertaken a number of international assignments to the US, Australia and South Africa but this was his first overseas assignment to Asia, and the first with his family, who had never lived outside of the UK.

Hong Kong was a very different assignment for John in comparison to his previous overseas postings. To begin with, he now ran a very diverse team, in terms of gender and ethnicity, compared to the ones he had been involved with before. John threw himself into work from day one but instead of focusing on what he had been tasked to deliver, he began to arrange meetings with the key partners in the firm, with no agenda other than getting to know his colleagues better. He also spent a considerable amount of time getting to know his own team, understanding their issues and challenges and trying to get some insights into some of the personalities involved in the firm's key clients. The first two months were spent investing time in some of his most important relationships, as well as socialising at dinners, sports clubs and other networking events to enable him to get himself known in Hong Kong. Yet while he was busy at the firm, he was still very concerned about how Anna and the children would integrate into this very alien environment for them. He need not have worried.

Before leaving for Hong Kong, Anna had conducted extensive research. Not only had she refined her choice of schools for the children down to a shortlist of two, but she had also investigated how to continue to pursue her own interests, in tennis and theatre, while overseas. She identified a number of tennis clubs and started exploring opportunities for amateur dramatics. On arrival in Hong Kong, she had selected the school and within two weeks had developed an extensive network with the mothers of her children's classmates, making sure to take the initiative and introduce herself to other parents and ask them for help. These new friends had been happy and eager to introduce her to the layout of Hong Kong and had spent time showing her around. They had been keen to discover what Anna's interests were and to help her find opportunities to explore those interests.

After three months both Anna and John felt very settled in Hong Kong thanks to their previous planning and their approach to building the right relationships, both personally and professionally. They had enjoyed a seamless integration into a new society and environment, which could have appeared quite intimidating had they not approached their posting in this way.

John and Anna were clear in their intentions from the outset – they wanted to make the most of their international posting and they didn't want to feel isolated, thousands of miles from their homes and families. John's experience and knowledge accumulated over a number of years was helpful, given the demands of his work, yet even so he didn't simply get on with the job; he sought to build great relationships, investing time in building broad networks first. Anna did the same, albeit with a different objective in mind – as this was her first time living abroad, she wanted to develop a strong and varied support network that she could call on if times were hard or she needed help when John was travelling.

Both followed the fundamental rules of networking:

- Be clear about the purpose of developing your network.

- Be specific about who you are targeting and their relevance to you.

- Give as well as take – always be prepared to reciprocate.

It would have been easy for John to focus solely on the day-to-day demands of his new role and for Anna simply to hope that she made local contacts once she was there, but their deliberate, targeted strategy paid dividends for them and made their new life much easier.

We all have social networks, some broader than others, some with deeper friendships than others. They fulfil our primal need to belong. We tend to build these networks intuitively, expanding them as opportunities and needs arise and losing touch with others as time passes. We manage these networks informally and without giving them too much thought; on the whole simply deriving satisfaction and pleasure from them.

The focus of this book, however, is networking in the professional sphere, although you'll likely find that many of the skills you need you will have already developed through your social networks. Networking is at the heart of business and should not be seen as a distracting waste of time, no matter what your role.

In their report 'How Leaders Create and Use Networks',* the academic Herminia Ibarra and journalist Mark Hunter suggest that to succeed, you need to build three types of network:

* *Harvard Business Review*, January 2007.

- **Operational:** people you need to accomplish your day-to-day job.

- **Personal:** kindred spirits outside your organisation who can help you with personal advancement.

- **Strategic:** planning for the future, using both your internal and external contacts to think about what you should be doing next.

While we would not disagree with Ibarra and Hunter, our view is that the three types of network are better defined as follows:

Personal	Internal	External
• To support your business and/or career development • To help you continue to learn new things • To support the development of your personal reputation and brand	• To help you in the delivery of your tasks and objectives for the organisation • To build breadth of personal support and sponsorship across the organisation beyond your area of responsibility • To develop 'followership' and engagement	• To obtain insights into future trends and developments in both your industry and the economy • To help spark ideas and seek innovation for your business or organisation • To support your ongoing professional development

Clearly, there is overlap between all three networks – you need to have people who can support you in your career in your personal, internal and external networks, for example – but the key issue is to recognise that this is why they are important to you, why you have invested time and effort in those relationships and why you need to keep in touch with them.

In the case of John and Anna, they were very focused on their personal and internal networks and the results were self-evident. Doubtless, with the benefit of having settled well, John would have turned his attention to external networking to further enhance his professional standing.

Personal networks

Whether you work in a large corporation or you own a small, entrepreneurial business, or whatever your employment situation, most people want to be successful – they want to progress in their career, be challenged by working on projects that 'stretch' them; they want their businesses to grow and flourish.

For those in corporations, most people would hope that their businesses are run on the basis of a meritocracy – that's to say that if you do a good job, then that success will be recognised and you will end up being promoted. You hope that by repeating your hard work and demonstrating your commitment, another promotion will then come your way. Yet the further up the organisation you go, the more competition there is for fewer senior positions; you can no longer rely on good work being recognised and rewarded, and must find new ways of making sure you stand out. There may also come a point when you decide that it is time to move on from that particular organisation in search of new opportunities.

It's before this point that you need to look at your personal network. As we have already stated, around two thirds of people find their next job through their own contacts, rather than through means such as job adverts or recruitment agencies. Your personal network will usually consist of friends and family, rather than current colleagues and business contacts, although there may also be overlap with people in your external network – mentors or coaches for example, or even recruiters, as they can support your development, as long as you are clear about what you want your next steps to be. A well-respected headhunter recently said:

'I get so fed up meeting bright, intelligent people who have no idea what they want to do. They make appointments to meet me, knowing that they want a new challenge in their career, but when I ask them about the characteristics of their next role, they often can't even tell me which sector they would like to work in let alone what job they are looking for. I had one person recently who said, and I quote: "I'd quite like to work in the drinks industry. But there again, manufacturing has always appealed to me and I have spent four years working in retail. My current colleague worked in pharmaceuticals and she really enjoyed that, so perhaps that might be interesting?"

They come expecting me to be the font of all knowledge and a bit of a mind reader as well – it drives me nuts! I'm never going to bother to see that person again and there is no chance that they will be going onto a short or long list of mine.'

So before having a conversation about your next career move, it is critical that you are clear about what that is – or at least that you have narrowed it down to two or three strong possibilities that you are committed to. Your pitch should be focused, clear and to the point, otherwise time spent with someone who could be enormously helpful will have been time wasted – yours and theirs.

A strong personal network can be beneficial in all sorts of ways in supporting and developing your career or business.

CASE STUDY

Jayne's mother was an entrepreneur. While she was at home raising her four children, she began making items to sell, such as aprons. Over the years the business grew, eventually supplying numerous high street stores, and during Jayne's younger years it became second nature to her to sit behind a sewing machine earning pocket money.

When Jayne had children of her own, before long she found herself using her skills on the sewing machine to make a variety of fancy dress costumes for her son and daughter. They became the envy of others in the nursery playground. As more and more parents began to ask Jayne where she bought the costumes, she had the genesis of a business idea: to take a leaf out of her mother's book and start making and selling a range of fancy dress outfits.

Jayne had a problem, however - she did not have the capacity to do larger scale manufacturing. Producing the odd costume wasn't a problem for her, but producing enough stock to supply shops was another thing altogether. Without the ability to scale up, the business would never grow.

She was discussing this issue one day while waiting to pick up her children from school with another parent, Mairi, who happened to be in the local Chamber of Commerce. Mairi suggested to Jayne that she talk to one of her colleagues who might be able to help. The next week Jayne met Mairi's contact for a cup of coffee and within a few days, Jayne had the names of three small businesses, each of which had the ability to help her with the production of costumes. The business was off the ground.

Jayne had been open to networking opportunities from any avenue, and was able to capitalise on her personal network to make a business idea become a reality.

Personal networks are also key to your personal development. It is important to continue to learn new skills and explore new interests, which may also prove useful for your continuous professional development. While some companies may assist with personal development plans, they often tend to be closely aligned with your current work objectives. Your personal network, on the other hand, is more likely to provide you with inspiration to try new things, broadening your experiences and knowledge.

How you act and behave outside of the work environment still has an impact on your overall personal brand, how you are perceived by people (see pages 96–98) – if you don't think that's the case then try googling yourself. See what emerges from your search and whether there are quotes, photos, Facebook posts or excerpts from your Twitter feed. Then check to see if these are the sorts of things that you want to be reflecting you professionally. We will be considering your online brand in Chapter 4, but for now it is important to ensure that your personal network consists of advocates for you, not detractors.

Internal networks

Most people are pretty good at internal networking. After all, the relationships in their internal networks are the ones that they have to maintain to get their job done, achieve their career and business objectives, and hopefully earn their rewards from. It is exceptionally hard to succeed in an organisation, no matter how large or small it is, unless you get on with your co-workers. You don't have to befriend them and include them in your social circle, but it is hugely helpful if you at least have a mutual respect for each other's professional expertise and technical know-how.

Such respect can emerge from your reputation – your standing in the industry or your personal presence and impact – but for most this is something that has to be actively developed. This can be relatively straightforward in many working environments because you may see many of your colleagues almost daily so relationships tend to develop as a matter of course, through catching up over coffee, having lunch together, or any of your daily workplace interactions. Almost by a process of osmosis, you can develop a network of good internal relationships. The question is, is this internal network broad enough and does it cover *all* the people that you may need to engage with or elicit support from? Similarly, if you invested time in a more structured approach, could you build a stronger internal network more quickly? After all, the stronger your network, the faster and more effective you can be at your job.

CASE STUDY

When two large organisations merged in the late nineties, there were some obvious benefits to be derived from crunching together two divisions with very similar products. One obvious place to make savings was in the area of procurement as both divisions bought many similar products, ranging from raw materials to packaging to the distribution of the finished goods. If better deals could be negotiated for 80 per cent of the overall spend, savings of around 20 to 25 per cent could be made – not an insignificant amount in an overall spend of approximately £900 million. The organisation decided to recruit a new team to develop a strategy, led by a procurement specialist named Brian, although he had never worked in the sector occupied by this newly merged organisation. Brian was the first to recognise that he had a very steep learning curve to negotiate. Picking his team itself was a challenging and time consuming activity but they eventually came from both the two merged organisations and from outside the business altogether.

They had a daunting task, especially given the pressure emerging from the shareholders of the merged organisation. The newly merged business also had manufacturing sites all over the world, including the Philippines, Brazil, America, Italy, the UK and Australia. So, rather than dive straight into strategy development, Brian spent the first four weeks or so of his new job on a plane, touring each and every one of the major manufacturing facilities, meeting his new colleagues and key stakeholders. He spent time with the local procurement teams, engaging them and explaining the principles of what he had been brought in to deliver. He met the General Managers of the various manufacturing plants, frequently dining with them so that they could have informal discussions over dinner and a glass of wine, but at the same time building a series of great relationships across the world. He knew that what he had been asked to do was bound to upset people because in negotiating great global deals for the organisation as a whole, Brian would likely impact or disadvantage some plants locally. He had to ensure that his key stakeholders in the regions recognised this and were prepared to support him when he encountered resistance.

Brian had invested his time well. When his new team developed their strategies for each of their areas, all of the resistance that Brian had anticipated started to emerge. But because he had spent time with the key people at each location, developing good relationships, it only took a phone call and things fell into place.

This is a classic case of a great internal network being established quickly in an organisation that Brian did not know and in a sector that he had absolutely no experience in. He understood what he needed to do and why – build a strong internal network of supporters first and foremost, before his team even contemplated addressing the task in hand – and developed a clear plan to execute his objectives. It was quite masterful and it wasn't surprising that Brian and his team over-delivered on their savings targets.

It may seem slightly contradictory, but your internal networks should also include people outside of your own organisation who are still critical to you achieving your goals. These people could be suppliers, customers or anyone else who may have an impact on your day-to-day work. Your interactions with these people will take place predominantly during working hours, and the key reason for interacting with them is to enable you to do your job effectively, so, as they are related to your job, but not strictly part of your organisation, you could call them your external/internal network.

These people can also be invaluable to have in your personal network. Suppliers to your organisation will very often be suppliers to your competitors and they will therefore be a very useful source of market intelligence, trends and the like. They may also be among the first to hear about new job opportunities that may arise – which may be of real personal benefit. If you do happen to move on, it is always worth keeping in touch with these sorts of people in the same way that you are well advised to keep in touch with former colleagues who move on – the 'alumni' population of organisations is a rich source for your networks.

Understanding the culture of an organisation is crucial when it comes to building an effective network, particularly in terms of communication. Some organisations run on emails. Others rely on face-to-face communication, either meetings in person or, if that's not possible, phone calls, videoconferences or Skype. Some people prefer to text while others use other communication tools such as WhatsApp. Some organisations love PowerPoint when presenting information, while others prefer printed handouts. Even those can vary – some may be restricted to a one-page summary, while others may consist of many pages of text. If your natural style is to write detailed prose and the organisation runs on PowerPoint, you will need to adapt your style quickly – or, at the very least, find someone who is a PowerPoint expert. The importance of understanding the working culture of an organisation should never be underestimated:

CASE STUDY

Andy joined a large international business as the Financial Controller. This organisation had a small Head Office in Manchester and large operational businesses in the Middle East, the USA and on mainland Europe. It was an organisation with a very distinctive culture centred on serving their customers exceptionally well, twenty four hours a day, seven days a week, 365 days a year. The people worked incredibly hard – and played just as hard. The organisation relied on its key people building exceptionally strong relationships, internally and externally.

When Andy joined, he spent some time trying to get to grips with this new culture. His predecessor had only lasted nine months before resigning and the Chief Financial Officer was keen for Andy not to go the same way. Andy's predecessor had made some fundamental errors when he joined: he had not understood the importance of the culture of round-the-clock service within the business; he had underestimated the importance placed on developing strong internal networks; and he had misread the preferred style of communication.

The CFO took time to explain this to Andy on his arrival and provided him with some very helpful pointers: meet and get to know his colleagues in the different regions, both professionally and socially; speak to them directly either in person, by phone or Skype, rather than written communication; appreciate the business culture and the work-hard-play-hard ethic. He told Andy, 'If you can make it past six months, you will be able to last a lifetime – but you will discover quickly whether this organisation is for you or not.'

Hard words perhaps, but it was advice that Andy took heed of. His early weeks were spent building a strong internal network and he adapted to the new culture, which he found very much to his liking, despite the cautionary words of the CFO. His first six months passed in a flash and after eighteen months in the organisation he was promoted into a new role overseas.

Developing strong interpersonal relationships in a business may sound obvious, but it is frequently taken for granted or seen as something 'nice to do'. There is a tendency for many people to focus solely on their job and, as a consequence, they tend to neglect the important tasks of managing relationships and stakeholders. Even those who do spend time on their internal networks, tend to focus on the obvious and closest relationships, which is a good start, but you will never go wrong establishing relationships as broadly as possible.

This is particularly important when considering the value of personal sponsorship in a business. Most people ensure that they have as good a relationship with their boss as possible – after all, the boss is responsible for your pay, so you don't want to upset them. This is all very well and good, but there may come a time when you would like to broaden your experience in the organisation and seek a new role. It is then that having a good breadth of support among your boss's peer group is very important. Decisions on promotion or secondments are rarely unilateral, so unless others have an opinion of you and your capabilities, you will only have one person, your line manager, fighting your corner.

So you should make the time to talk to your boss's peer group – something that a lot of people find difficult to do. After all, why should someone who may have no interest in what you are doing take the time to meet and talk to you?

You need to think about what the hook could be for initiating conversations with them, because once you are in front of them, you have a golden opportunity to impress. Consider this: if you had to find not one, but several referees for yourself and you had to choose them from senior colleagues, firstly, who would you choose and, secondly, what do you think they would say about you? If you cannot list more than three people, then you have a challenge on your hands and if you don't know what they would say about you, that is even more of a problem.

CASE STUDY

Gill had been working for Adam for four years in the same role and she had been doing an excellent job. She remained ambitious for herself in her career and she had a hankering to work in another division in the company, hopefully in a more senior role. Adam was a strong advocate for her, but she wasn't well known by others in Adam's peer group or indeed, by anyone else higher up in the business.

One day she was talking to John, a friend who had, from time to time, offered her career advice. 'I really love this business and I'd love to do something else in a different division that plays to my technical expertise, but I don't know how to go about it. What should I do?' Gill asked him.

John's counsel was very straightforward: 'You can't just rely on Adam to fight your corner – you have to begin to talk to some others in the organisation who will recognise what you are capable of and you will have to trust in them to become your advocates.'

Not being a natural networker, it was as if she was going to have to become someone else to do this most daunting of tasks, yet a task that was going to be crucial for her career. Eventually she came up with a great metaphor to enable her to get into the right mind-set for the task at hand: 'I'm going to put on my peacock suit and just do it.'

Gill identified four people that she felt were very influential in the organisation and found a variety of different reasons to go and talk to each of them in turn. Having arranged appointments, she 'put on her peacock suit' and started networking. Nine months later, she achieved her ambition, leaving Adam, with his blessing, to move into another role in the organisation where she became well regarded and successful. But she did not discard her 'peacock suit' – her networking became a part of what she did as a matter of course and it continues to contribute to her very successful career.

So far we have talked about building good internal networks up (with your boss and their peer group) and out (with other key stakeholders that you have cause to interact with and need support from). We have not talked about networking down. 'That's obvious – that's leadership!' might be your immediate reaction and you would be right. Great leaders create follower-ship from their teams, yet for most great leaders this is not intuitive – they have to work on it. Charisma and personality will get you so far, but if you scratch the surface and that is all you find, it will not be long before the lack of substance in that leader is exposed.

So, good leadership relies on building good networks down-wards as well as out and up, investing time in your people and key lieutenants. Followership is founded on mutual respect and not necessarily friendship; you cannot always be friends with your colleagues but you do need to respect them.

Leaders who create great followership more often than not have well-developed emotional intelligence. Emotional intelligence is a much-used term, and yet few understand what it constitutes.

The term originated with psychologists John Mayer and Peter Salovey in their paper in 1990, although Israeli psychologist Reuven Bar-On had developed a concept that he called 'Emotional Quotient' in 1985. The phrase 'Emotional Intelligence' was then popularised by the American journalist, Daniel Goleman, in his book of the same name. This model of Emotional Intelligence has been further developed by psychologist Martyn Newman into key elements, which are:

Self-awareness	Self-knowing
	Straightforwardness
Self-management	Self-control
	Self-confidence
	Self-reliance
Social Awareness	Empathy
Social Skills	Relationship skills
Adaptability	Adaptability
	Optimism
	Self-actualisation

Delving into the realms of emotional intelligence is another matter altogether, so for now we would simply like to bring it to your attention. It is something that you should consider; think about how you could work on any of the facets that might be underdeveloped in yourself. Suffice to say, creating good networks is easier if you are emotionally intelligent:

CASE STUDY

The CEO of a large division of a multinational business had a reputation for being somewhat irascible. If he was in a bad mood at meetings, he would tear strips off his team at the drop of a hat, and more junior managers were terrified if they had to present at meetings that he was chairing, lest they bore the brunt of his sharp tongue.

On the floor that he worked, his was the only cellular office – the remaining staff worked outside it in an open-plan environment. As his division was located on the fifth floor, most people took the lifts rather than used the stairs. But when this particular person emerged from the lift, everyone else would pick up the phones and pretend to dial or immerse themselves in some detailed report in order to avoid eye contact and the possibility that he might bark something in their direction.

Unsurprisingly to many, this particular CEO had one falling out too many and he parted company with the organisation in the weeks before the Christmas break. His successor was appointed almost immediately. David came from another part of the business, and he was expected to start on the first working day in January.

When David emerged from the lifts onto the fifth floor on his first day, instead of walking to the office, he stopped where the opening from the lifts met the open-plan office floor and in a loud voice, boomed:

'Hi there everyone. My name is David and I'm really excited to be working here with you all. I hope you had a fantastic Christmas and New Year with your families – it's going to be a really busy year in our division, so with any luck your batteries will be fully charged and you will be ready to go. I'm looking forward to meeting you all over the next few days to hear about what you have been up to and how we can really do something special in this division this year. Let's have our best year yet!'

And with that, he walked to his office. In an instant, the atmosphere on the floor had changed from one of fear and trepidation to genuine excitement. Instead of people avoiding eye contact with their boss, they actively looked to engage with David whenever he emerged from the lifts. Good to his word, he spent time with everyone, having one-to-one meetings, understanding their issues and challenges and thereby began to build his network downwards and create followership from his new team.

It was their best year ever under David's management, and he has since gone on to be the CEO of two FTSE-100 companies.

There was no doubt that David had well-developed emotional intelligence and he used that to create really strong follower-ship with his team. He was not a leader who shirked from taking difficult decisions about the business or people, but he always managed decisions in a humane way. He invested time in all of his people, but in particular with his team of direct reports and their teams as well – he spanned the whole organisation so that his well-honed, characterful leadership touched everyone.

Some managers and leaders are great at focusing on objectives and tasks; they may be highly effective leaders with well-developed emotional intelligence and their teams may be great at delivering for them, yet often this is without making use of strong interpersonal relationships. As Ibarra and Hunter said: 'Many managers do not immediately grasp that this will involve relational – not analytical – tasks. Nor do they easily understand that exchanges and interactions with a diverse array of current and potential stakeholders are not distractions from their "real work" but are actually at the heart of their new leadership roles.'

So creating strong internal networks is crucial to success – and thinking about the directions of your networks can be helpful to provide you with a structured approach:

Upwards: with your boss and his or her peer group.

Outwards: with some of your key internal and external stakeholders.

Downwards: with your people to create followership.

Across: with your own peer group.

Internal networking is part of doing your job – but doing your job can be so much easier with excellent internal networks.

External networks

The eighteenth century in Scotland is known as the period of The Scottish Enlightenment. It is the time when some of the great Scottish 'thought leaders' – economists, philosophers and the like – would come together to debate and discuss ideas. People like Adam Smith (author of *The Wealth of Nations*), David Hume (whose great work was *A Treatise of Human Nature*) and others such as James Hutton, Robert Adam, Alison Rutherford and Joseph Black, all came to prominence during the mid-eighteenth century. These Scottish scholars, intellectuals and thinkers spent their time in clubs, taverns and at dinner discussing and debating ideas and concepts about the future in all sorts of different fields. They were networking. Their legacy has been transformational.

Connecting with people outside of your usual set of colleagues and acquaintances is where most folk tend to struggle. They don't make time to do this, either because they fail to understand how it might prove useful or they may simply not know where to start. Yet as with building strong personal and internal networks, the rules for establishing and maintaining external networks are the same. Firstly, you have to be clear about the purpose of your networking and secondly, you need a clear understanding of where you go to build these networks. We will come to the second point in the next chapter. The purpose of building a strong network outside of your organisation and outside of your personal network is threefold:

1. To obtain insights into future trends and developments in both your industry and the economy

2. To help spark ideas and seek innovation for your business or organisation

3. To support your ongoing professional development and learning

Now, clearly there is going to be overlap in your networks and some people will appear in your personal and external networks, while some will feature in your internal and personal networks – that doesn't matter. What is important is that you give some consideration to the future and the implications for you and your business.

Let's consider the first point – how to obtain insights into future trends and developments in your industry and the economy. The world is littered with great businesses that didn't do that. In 1992, the CEO of Nokia, Jorma Ollila, made a decision to concentrate exclusively on telecommunications. The organisation was a classic Finnish conglomerate whose origins dated back to 1865 and over the years it had interests in a wide variety of businesses, from rubber to cabling to electricity generation, to name but three. Nokia was a trailblazer in the mobile phone industry and the Nokia ringtone, launched in 1994, was its trademark – when it was heard, people reached for their pockets the length and breadth of the land to check if it was their phone ringing, such was its popularity. Nokia was responsible for introducing text messaging to mobile phones in 1993, and in 1998, it was the largest phone manufacturer in the world, dwarfing Motorola, Samsung, Apple and Sony. Yet when the iPhone appeared on the scene in 2007 with a different operating system from Nokia, the tide began to turn. Indeed, both Android and iOS began to overtake Nokia's Symbian system and popularity of the ubiquitous phones began to wane. In 2011, Nokia entered a partnership with Microsoft and in 2013 it was announced that Microsoft was acquiring Nokia's mobile business; Nokia's previous market dominance was over.

So what has this to do with networking, you might wonder. Nokia didn't appreciate that instead of making phones, it was making devices with a breadth of functionality that may have seemed impossible to imagine, and that is what caused it to fail – just as Kodak failed to adapt to the digital revolution in cameras, despite having invented the core technology used in digital cameras.

Had the company's executives paid more attention to what was happening outside their business rather than inside it, things might have been different. That might be over-simplifying things, but identifying future trends is key to business success, and an important part of that is having a great external network. You have to be curious about future economic and social trends: what is happening with technology and how that is impacting on how we all live today? Trying to discover 'what's next?' isn't easy, but if you look outside of your business or organisation, you are much more likely to find the answer.

One large organisation in the UK has set up a mentoring scheme. That's not rocket science, you might think, but this is a reverse mentoring scheme and instead of older, more senior managers mentoring youngsters, it is the youngsters who are mentoring the older and more senior executives. They are sharing how they communicate, what they are interested in, and what trends are emerging among their friends. With the pace of change accelerating, future trends are more likely to be spotted first by a different generation from those who shape and define the strategy of big organisations. This scheme is a brilliant idea and a great example of how to create a different network.

The key question for many is where to go to obtain these insights and ideas – and that in itself requires some creativity, but investing the time to think about who might introduce you to whom is the first step in the process.

When writing this book, we wanted to provide our readers with tools to enhance their networking activities. An idea emerged that this could be facilitated by an app – and so BizPrompt was conceived (see pages 201–202). The question then arose, how could we get this developed and who might do it for us? Through our network, we knew of one app developer who had created something similar, so we set up a meeting. That didn't work out, but we were able to try another contact already in our network, and soon the app was in development.

In this case, we were fortunate to already have the right contacts in our networks – the same could be said of our connection to our publishers – and they are now firmly in our internal network as well.

If you don't already have the right contacts in your network, it can be a challenge to know where to start. Some large organisations have their own innovation divisions, others outsource their creativity to agencies, but most have to rely on the grey matter of their employees. And, of course, some people tend to be more creative than others, while some are great at building on ideas rather than coming up with the original idea itself.

It is important that you create the right environment to be creative – an environment that stimulates all of your senses – and that you bring diversity of thinking into a group in all its shapes and forms. Networking is about connecting with the right people to help your business flourish.

Finally, your external network is key to your own personal development and learning. A renowned headhunter once said that she always asks candidates whether they feel they have the right skills and expertise to do the job she is recruiting for. If they say 'yes' and that they have all the experience they need, garnered over years, then she discounts them and doesn't even put them on the long list. If, on the other hand, they tell her that they have learned a lot in their time in work and expect to continue to learn in the new role, then she is much more inclined to consider them serious candidates for the role.

Curiosity is a valuable quality and incredibly useful when net-working. Curiosity will help you enquire properly of your contacts and connections; it will help you seek out interesting individuals to bring into your network and it will assist you in learning and developing on a personal front. Curiosity will also help you draw parallels between other businesses and organisations and your own; investigate new technologies and how they may help you or what you are doing and it will also help you seek out interesting opportunities for yourself in your career.

Having a broad external network is also very helpful when you decide to move on from your current organisation. Former colleagues, bosses, suppliers, advisors and customers are often incredibly valuable sources of connections even if they are not immediately helpful themselves. As we keep saying – and it bears repeating – two thirds of people find their next opportunity from within their own networks, therefore the broader the external network, the greater the opportunity.

SUMMARY

▶ Consider your network in three dimensions: personal, internal and external. Be clear about what you want from each of those three networks and why – aimless networking is hugely time-consuming for all parties concerned and only occasionally leads to valuable connections.

▶ Networking can be daunting, but it need not be if you approach it in a methodical way, with real intent and purpose. It does require an investment of time and effort but the payback is definitely worth it.

Getting Started with Networking

KEY POINTS

▶ Evaluate the current state of your existing network with a thorough audit of your existing contacts.

▶ Prioritise the people in each of your categories.

▶ Consider how you will make time for networking going forward.

▶ Decide where the gaps are in your network and consider how to fill them, using existing contacts and identifying new ones.

Doing something new is often a bit terrifying. Whether it is learning to dance, figuring out how to operate a new phone, or trying to master a language, it's often a steep learning curve and many people are gripped with trepidation rather than excitement. All sorts of fears and self-doubts emerge: will I make myself look stupid and dance as if I have two left feet?

How come my teenage children can master this technology and find all the shortcuts faster than I can? Does my accent sound ridiculous to a native speaker?

The same applies to networking – it can appear very intimidating at first when you want to start expanding networks. People experience a range of insecurities: where do I start? How do I go about making contact? What happens if people don't respond to my invitations? How do I make myself interesting to them? All valid anxieties, yet you have to remember that you have spent your whole life networking to some extent, even if not deliberately. You most likely already have at least some form of personal, internal and external networks in place, so you're not starting from scratch, merely looking to expand networks that already exist.

The difference is that, to date, you have been networking without clarity of purpose. You have not intended to develop your networks – they have developed naturally through your day-to-day social and professional interactions. You have not done anything with them because (a) you have not thought about them in that way and (b) you have not properly understood how they might be able to help you.

So while the task of networking may appear overwhelming at first, it can be broken down into some simple, manageable steps:

1. You need to know where you are.

2. You need to figure out where you want to be and develop a plan to get there.

3. You need to turn that plan into action.

CASE STUDY

Joanna was a successful entrepreneur. Having graduated from university, she joined a recruitment company as a researcher. It wasn't long before her hard work and capability were recognised and she progressed very quickly, being promoted to an associate to help with search and selection assignments. Although she was being fast-tracked to become a partner, she decided that she wanted to run her own recruitment business, so she left and within twelve months had set up her own organisation.

Joanna's business grew very quickly – she won a variety of new contracts from large organisations and the company became increasingly profitable. During this time she met and married her husband and, five years after she had founded her business, she made a life-changing decision. She started a family and sold her company, having two children in quick succession almost immediately following the sale.

But as the children began to reach nursery and school age, Joanna began to get fidgety and had the urge to go back into business.

This time, she decided to start a sales training organisation, as that was one of her core skills and something that she was well known for. The structure and product were relatively straightforward for Joanna to deal with – what was lacking was her network.

The first thing that she did was write down a long list of all of her contacts and connections from all her walks of life – her former business, her education, other mums, neighbours, friends from her sports clubs and any other contacts she could think of. She then began to research where they worked and what they did, predominantly through LinkedIn. When she found them, she invited them to connect with her. Once connected, she arranged a series of meetings, and before long, Joanna had established her second business and work was beginning to flow in. Joanna also joined an organisation for entrepreneurs and actively sought out other organisations that could help her connect with like-minded folk.

Despite having neglected a very well-established professional network for over five years, Joanna was still able to reinvigorate it and turn it into a network that was every bit as useful and vibrant as before.

Joanna was very clear about what she needed to do and how to go about doing it, not least because she had been a consummate networker in her days as a recruitment consultant, but she still followed a structured process to restart her network.

Let's look at each of those steps in turn.

How good is your network?

Step one is all about understanding just how well developed your network is at the moment. To do this, you need to ask yourself three questions:

1. Who are the people in your network?

2. Why are these people in your network?

3. What would make your network better?

We will consider how you audit your network more comprehensively a little later on, but in posing yourself these three questions, you should begin to get some insights into the challenges that are likely to lie ahead.

Who are the people in your network?

It may sound like an obvious point, but you need to know who you know. You should have a good idea of the size of your network but you need to be really specific about who these people are. You also need to know what roles each person plays in your network – we'll look at why you know them when we tackle the next question but it's important to be clear about this.

Does your network consist of thirty people (probably too small) or 300 people (probably too large)? We will look at what is the sensible size of a network later in the chapter (see pages 45–50) but for now, we simply need to get a rough idea of the size. How many people do you know and, importantly, keep in touch with regularly – whether it is once a week, once a quarter or once a year? Anyone you are in touch with less frequently than that should not be counted at all – they are merely acquaintances so do not include them in your network.

Now we know how large your network is, we need to establish why it is that you consider these people important enough to be in your network.

Why are these people in your network?

On the basis that we are considering your business networks only at this point, the answer to this question should be straightforward. People in your network should be there because they match the objectives of one of the three types of network: personal, internal and external (see page 7).

If you have a long list of people who you connect with frequently but who don't fulfil any one of the networks' criteria, you really should be asking yourself 'Why are these people in my business network and why do I keep in touch with them?' If you cannot answer these questions with absolute clarity, then these people do not belong in your network. By all means, connect with them socially, but you are wasting your time connecting with them for work purposes.

You should also be giving some thought to how the people in your business network reflect you and your personal brand. What does your connection to them say about you? What do they think about you and what do they know and say about you? We have talked about the need to have a number of people who are your personal ambassadors and advocates in the previous chapter – if you don't already, you should give some thought as to who might be able to do this for you:

CASE STUDY

Stephen works in the drinks industry. At one point in his career, he worked on a special project for which he reported directly to the CEO, even though he worked in a different division and was significantly more junior that his new temporary boss. Stephen did an excellent job with the project and during the course of that work, developed a great rapport with the CEO.

When the task had been completed, the CEO said: 'Stephen, I'd like to keep in touch with you and help you with your career if I can – let's keep in touch and get together every six to nine months or so for a chat.'

This was 'manna from heaven' for Stephen and an offer too good to refuse. Even though he left that particular organisation, the CEO (who has since also left to become a Chairman of a number of different companies) has remained good to his word and continues to act as a mentor and guide to Stephen and has counselled him since they first met.

What would make your network better?

At this point, having established who is in your network and why, it's time to give some thought to what would make it better still and, again, you have to ask yourself some questions.

What areas of your network need to be worked on, personal, internal or external? Is your network too small and does it need to be expanded? Is your network too large and does it need to be pared down? (See pages 45–46.) Who else should you be connecting with and why will they help you? If you don't know them, who do you know who might and can they introduce you?

Start thinking in a systematic way about what you need to do next – and at this point, you need to remind yourself again why you're doing this. What are your priorities? Is it about getting your job done, meeting your objectives, and working more efficiently and effectively? Is it about future-proofing your business? Or is it about you and your career – making that next move? Focus is a key part of effective networking.

So, let's look at your network in a little more detail.

Auditing your current network

There are three key points to consider when it comes to auditing a network:

1. **Classification:** know who is in your network, which of your networks they exist in and how important those networks are to you.

2. **Prioritisation:** once you have classified the people in your network, prioritise their importance to you and decide how frequently you would like to interact with them.

3. **Planning**: establish how much time you devote to networking and, more importantly, how much time you are able to allocate to networking in the future.

Classification

We would recommend using the table opposite to help classify your network.

Once you start listing all your contacts, it may surprise you the number of people that you know when you really think about it. Some may be closer friends, colleagues or acquaintances than others, but we all know a lot more people than we can remember off the top of our heads.

Of course, the list of people might not be the ideal current network for you or you might realise that it needs some work and we will address that later, but for now we need to figure out what to do with this list of names, and how to manage it. To do that we have to look at the priorities in our network and think about how frequently we contact everyone.

Prioritisation

We have already done some prioritising into our categories 1, 2 and 3, so now we have to cross-check whether our initial

Names	Classification	Prioritisation
In this column, list all the people in your network currently. They could come from: • School • University • Home and social contacts • Sporting clubs • Current work colleagues • Former work colleagues • Suppliers and other contacts outside your own organisation • Interests and hobbies outside of work • Professional bodies • Networking organisations • LinkedIn • Other online networks	Having made a long list of contacts, assign them to your personal, internal or external networks. If you cannot classify everyone in your list of names, they should not be on the list – by all means keep in touch with them, but on a social basis, not for work.	Having identified which of your networks everyone belongs to (some can be in more than one), prioritise their importance to you. We suggest three categories (e.g. 1, 2 and 3, with 1 being the most important to you, and 3 the least important).

prioritisation reflects how often we are in touch with the people in our networks. We need to do this for each of our networks. Time for another table, this time listing when we were last in touch with each of our contacts and when we plan to contact them again:

Personal Network			
Category	Name	Last Contact	Next Planned Contact
1	Joe Brandon	12 Sept	14 Oct
	Sarah Smith	30 Aug	2 Oct
	Jenny Milton	3 Sept	10 Oct
2	Darren Fox	9 July	15 Oct
	Jim Brown	21 June	20 Sept
3	Jane Billings	3 March	4 Sept
	David Niven	12 May	20 Nov

Internal Network			
Category	Name	Last Contact	Next Planned Contact
1			
2			
3			

External Network			
Category	Name	Last Contact	Next Planned Contact
1			
2			
3			

Let's assume it is currently mid-September. We have been in touch with each of our personal contacts over the previous six months or so and we have planned to contact them again within a pre-determined timeframe. For the Category One contacts, it is once a month; for the Category Two contacts, it is once a quarter and for the Category Three contacts, we are in touch with them twice a year.

You may have noted that we did not say that we met each of these contacts, but that we had 'been in touch' with them and this is a very important point. If we have 150 to 200 people in our various networks (which isn't unreasonable) we would spend our lives firstly trying to arrange meetings with these people and secondly spending time having cups of coffee or tea with them, and clearly this is impractical. We will talk about how to stay in touch with our networks later, but it is simply that – staying in touch. What's more, even though we might be wonderfully diligent with our plans to contact everyone in our networks, they may be in touch with us on a different frequency. Someone who may be a Category Three contact for us may suddenly connect with us only a matter of weeks after we were last in touch with them, in which case we can push our 'connecting' date back by six months or so. This may sound slightly complicated to keep track of, but if you do find it tricky, our BizPrompt app has been designed specifically to manage this challenge automatically, and we will cover how it works at the end of the book (see pages 201–202). For now, we are bringing structure and order to the process of networking and once that has been established, it should be relatively straightforward to maintain.

We have classified our network and we have prioritised. Now we need to plan how much time we can devote to networking.

Planning
There are 168 hours in a week. This means that apart from time when you might be asleep, say for 56 of those hours,

there are around 112 hours in which you have an opportunity to do some networking. 'But that includes the weekends!' you might argue – but remember, you have a personal network as well as an internal and external network so why not make use of all the time that is available to you?

The working day may last from 8.30 a.m. to 5.30 p.m., but there is always time to network before or after work as well as during the day. Breakfasts and early evening drinks or dinners are perfect opportunities to network and those who are best at networking make use of all the time they are awake to do it. For them, it is a way of life rather than an additional chore. So you need to understand how much time you spend networking currently and also think about how much time you *could* spend networking. If you were to populate the table below, what would it look like?

Day of the week:

	Morning (before work)	Working Day	Evening (after work)
Personal Network	*Insert time spent networking*		
Internal Network			
External Network			

In our experience, most people will populate the middle box of the table, i.e. there will be lots of networking done during the working day with people in their internal network. It's not surprising that this is the case, because if we don't do what we need to do at work, we run the risk of getting fired or our business failing. Yet if it is only the middle box of the table that has meetings listed in it, think of the opportunities that you have to grow and develop your networks more broadly.

Planning, therefore, means looking at where the opportunities lie to invest time in networking. Take the daily table and extend it for the whole week and think about what you might be able to fit in – a couple of breakfast meetings, a meeting or two after work and already your networks could be growing at an exponential rate:

CASE STUDY

In his late thirties, David decided that it was time for a change of career. He had worked for the same organisation for more than a decade, but even in his youth he had wanted to run his own business. The time had come to take the big step away from corporate life. Over the years he had accumulated enough experience to put together a compelling consultancy offering. Although he was returning to his home town, he had not given any consideration to how he was going to sell his services. He knew that it was going to take time to get his business up and running, and that first he needed to activate his network.

He began by listing the people he knew in his home town, beginning with his former colleagues from his previous job, then, working backwards chronologically, colleagues from former employers, university and even school. He thought about other organisations – a rugby club, a cricket club and even his school old boys club. After he had trawled through his network of friends, he thought about how they might be able to help him, but also, how he might be able to help them in return to encourage good will.

He had a list of seventy to eighty names, but little idea of how to prioritise them so he began to contact them all. He spent time chatting to each of them and once he had his first discussion he then prioritised each one, making a note of when to contact them next. Most importantly, he was quick to follow up with a note thanking them for their time. At the end of each meeting, he asked the same question: 'Who else do you know who might be interested in hearing about what I'm up to?'

In asking the simplest of questions, almost always he was given the names of at least two more people to connect with and so David grew his network quickly and effectively. Applying the same process to his new connections, it wasn't long before the business was thriving – he had beaten his start up goals with a well-developed network of over 150 supporters and advocates of his new business.

David followed some of the main principles of networking:

- He approached the task systematically, clear about what he was trying to achieve.

- He engaged with people, offering something as well as asking for help.

- He followed up with everyone quickly.

- He asked everyone for help in developing his network.

A fundamental question remains: are your networking efforts well directed? To answer this question, we have to consider what the audit of our network told us. Is our network the right size, does it have the right balance and are we interacting with it in the right way?

What is the ideal size of a network?

Working in the 1990s, anthropologist Robin Dunbar suggested that the brain can only manage a limited number of social relationships comfortably – he concluded that number was around 150.

Dunbar was conducting research into non-human primates and their grooming habits, and he decided to extend his hypothesis into the realm of social groups for humans. He was investigating the idea that the size of the neocortex in the brain and its processing ability is the limiting factor in determining group size, and that led him to the figure of 150. Other surveys appear to support this, ranging from village and tribe sizes to the basic unit size of armies in Roman times.

As defined in the Oxford English Dictionary, Dunbar's number is: A theoretical limit to the number of people with whom any individual is able to sustain a stable or meaningful social relationship (usually considered to be roughly 150).

Defined another way, it is a suggested cognitive limit to the number of people with whom one can maintain stable social relationships. These are relationships in which an individual knows who each person is and how each person relates to every other person.

This second definition would suggest that there is some depth to a relationship and that it goes beyond being a mere acquaintance or connection online. There should be some substance to the way in which you both interact and a knowledge of each other that is more than simply superficial.

Since then, other researchers have proposed that the number actually lies between 150 and 250. There may be some grounds to argue whether the 'right' number is 150, 200 or 250 but what is certain is that it is hard to have good-quality relationships with an enormous number of people – you simply do not have enough hours in the day to maintain them, particularly if those relationships require some depth.

In defining the size of your own networks, you need to be aware of a number of different factors, such as the number, quality and depth of the relationships that you need to nurture (which will depend on your own situation), not to mention your own priorities. Are you thinking of moving jobs? Do you need support in delivering your objectives or business plan? Do you need to future proof your business?

Knowing where you currently stand is the starting point. You should be able to summarise your current networks in a table, similar to the one below – let's take the situation of David from the last case study and look at the situation when he started up his new consultancy business (see opposite).

David's largest network was his personal network as it consisted of his friends as well as colleagues who had become friends from previous jobs. They were all key acquaintances, at least until he had been able to classify them more effectively.

He had a very small internal network when he started: a handful of people that he had trained with and talked about

	Category	Current Number	Total	Desired Number	Total
Personal network	1	34			
	2	10	48		
	3	4			
Internal network	1	4			
	2	2	6		
	3				
External network	1	8			
	2	10	20		
	3	2			

connecting with to do associate work, and no customers or suppliers at all. This was where he needed to develop his network – and fast.

There were a few people in his external network that he kept in touch with from time to time, some more frequently than others. Some of these people were competitors and some were individuals that he had come across who worked in areas complementary to his own. Some were subject matter experts that he could call on from time to time for advice and there were a couple of his former mentors who had also moved on from his previous organisation but had kept in touch.

Just by looking at the table, he knew he had to rebalance it; he had far too many contacts in his personal network and although they were all priority one for him at the moment, he recognised that this would not be productive in the long term. His internal, work-related network was to be his main priority and he had to think about how he could develop this quickly. He decided that he wanted to have around 150 people in his network to be able to manage it effectively – around Dunbar's number:

	Category	Current Number	Total	Desired Number	Total
Personal network	1	34		8	
	2	10	48	15	30
	3	4		7	
Internal network	1	4		30	
	2	2	6	50	105
	3			25	
External network	1	8		4	
	2	10	20	8	15
	3	2		3	

David knew that he needed the majority of his network to be in his internal network and felt that about 70 per cent of his total network should be about right. Some of his old personal network migrated into his internal network, those who were able to provide professional support for him, but the majority of the people that ended up in his internal network were new to him.

He also tried to prioritise his network in a way that would make managing it relatively simple and straightforward. So, he decided that he should have around thirty priority one contacts – his logic being that he could contact one a day over the course of a month. He could have tried to force more contacts into his priority one category, but he felt that this would make it hard to balance his work with his business development activity. With the rest of his network, his intention was to contact his priority two contacts once a quarter and his priority three contacts twice a year and so he set about re-balancing his intended and ideal network to the numbers seen in the 'desired number' column in the table above.

Applying similar logic to his personal and external networks, he was able to make a plan to go about building a comprehensive group of people to support him and his new business.

You will see that roughly 30 per cent of David's desired number is priority one contacts, around 50 per cent priority two contacts and the remainder is priority three, which from a practical perspective made sense for him. When planning your own network, you will have to work out the right balance for you. It may be worth seeking some help and advice on this, but as a guideline, a 1:2:1 ratio of priority one, priority two and priority three contacts is not a bad rule of thumb to get you started. If you have around 150 people in your network, the 1:2:1 ratio gives you a number of 38:75:38 (or thereabouts). This means that, roughly speaking, you would have to contact one priority one contact a day and one priority two contact a day, leaving you one priority three contact to connect with each week. Of course, these numbers are approximate but will help guide you so that your networking efforts are evenly spread and not overwhelming, so you don't have to contact too many people at a time.

Of course, what is right for you now may not be right for you in the future and this is a very important point. Networks are dynamic, fluid things – you will constantly be adding, removing and reprioritising people from your network depending on your situation and the state of your career or business, to keep your network as relevant as possible. Remember, you only have a limited number of waking hours in the week and you need to make the best use of them.

Building your network

So, you have done an audit on your network and you have decided it needs some attention. You have looked at your diary and have worked out that you can find a few more hours in the week to spend networking both during the working day and outside of conventional working hours. You are clear about why you need to develop your network and, specifically, the areas where your network is deficient. You understand that your network is going to be limited in number and size and that you will need to manage it well.

But where do you start? How do you go about building your network? It's hard enough developing it at work before you even give any consideration to an external network.

One of the key things is to remain focused. The worst thing you can do is take a scattergun, random approach to developing your network, adding anyone and everyone to your list of contacts. Remember why you are doing this – it is to do one of three things:

1. To build a network that will help you in your career and your learning and development.

2. To develop a network that will enable you to get things done more effectively and efficiently in your organisation.

3. To ensure you have a network or business that helps you focus on the future as well as the here and now.

If you find yourself adding people to your network that do not fit into any one of the groups above then you really shouldn't be including them – recalibrate your efforts and begin again.

When you are beginning, it is too easy to get over enthusiastic and build too big a network of people, all of whom you consider to be in your priority one set of contacts. This will leave you overstretched and will detract from your ability to prioritise effectively, so we would recommend that you follow three easy steps:

1. Prioritise where you want to grow your network and decide on the size you would ideally like it to be.

2. Start small – begin by developing some really good contacts in all three categories and manage them really well.

3. Grow your network gradually from this solid foundation.

You will find it considerably easier to manage things in this way. It will also enable you to get used to the rhythm of networking and for it to become a way of working rather than something that seems like a difficult task in addition to your everyday work. Networking should be part of your daily life. Once you get into the habit of networking it will become intuitive and natural to do. Even enjoyable.

Remember that networks are fluid – people join them and exit from them – so some contacts you make now may not be relevant to you at this moment, but they may be at some point in the future:

CASE STUDY

Tim, a management consultant, met Angela through a colleague of his. Angela was very senior in her organisation and was doing some work with Tim's colleague. When they met on a couple of occasions they got on very well, but neither thought of incorporating the other into their network.

Over ten years later, Tim met Angela again at another social event. They remembered each other and took up from where they had left off. Angela had since left the organisation where she was working when they first met and was now CEO of another large business. Tim asked if she was still working with his former colleague and Angela said no. Instead she asked Tim to come along for a coffee one day to discuss some of her current business challenges and whether Tim might be able to help – it was almost an open invitation to do some business together.

A number of weeks later they met and Angela was as good as her word – Tim secured some work, was introduced to some of Angela's key staff members and struck up a long-standing working relationship with the firm, even though Angela subsequently retired to pursue a plural career. Tim and Angela kept in touch and Angela was kind enough to introduce Tim to a business where she was Chair, which led to even more work for Tim. The most bizarre connection came, however, when Angela was being entertained at the theatre by Jeff, a competitor from her former industry.

She mentioned Tim, and discovered that he and Tim were neighbours but had never met. Angela connected them both and they established a new relationship.

Angela was a consummate networker – she recognised that sometimes things need not develop but may do as time passes; she was always aware of the opportunity. She also played the roles of Giver, Taker and Connector in networking, connecting two people even though she had nothing directly to gain – one of the attributes of an experienced networker. Doubtless she would get some benefit further down the line as either Tim or Jeff would connect her with someone in their networks.

As well as demonstrating that you never know when a contact will become highly relevant to your network, the above case study brings us to another key point: the roles to play when networking. The very best networkers will always do the following:

1. Offer to do something for the counterparty (Giver)

2. Ask for something from the counterparty (Taker)

3. Connect the counterparty with other useful contacts (Connector)

Sometimes you will end up playing all three roles at the same time, but you should always aim to fulfil all three at some point during every relationship. When building your network you will more often than not be the Taker in the conversation but even if you are receiving, you should still always offer to help. The Giver may not need anything from you right now, but they are building up credit with you for help or support at some time in the future, even if it is only to see if you can connect them with someone who might be helpful.

Let's consider each of these roles in more detail:

Giver: Offering something in a conversation is a golden rule in networking. Whether you are giving advice, offering support or being prepared to connect someone to another person in your network, it is really important always to ask 'Is there anything I can do to help you?' at the end of a conversation. More often than not, in making yourself available for a conversation you have already demonstrated that you are a Giver, which is a great start, but if you have begun the discussion playing a different role, you must remember that networking is about creating mutual benefits.

Taker: When beginning your networking journey, this is the role that you are most likely to play. You will be asking someone for a favour, to join your network or asking them to connect you to someone that they know. This can feel selfish and awkward. We need a certain amount of self-confidence to ask for something without the fear of being rejected and this is a barrier that many struggle to overcome.

Connector: These people are alive to opportunities and have subsets in their networks, which they use to great effect to join people up. They are always thinking of areas of joint interest, not only with the people that they are talking to in the moment, but also in relation to their networks. They are looking for opportunities to link people up wherever they are. It is easier to be a Connector in an internal network (i.e. within an organisation); the best Connectors make linkages constantly throughout all of their networks.

Building from the inside out

In 1929 a Hungarian author, Frigyes Karinthy, wrote a short story called *Chains*. In the short story he proposed that anyone in the world could be connected to another person by six steps, or introductions by a friend of a friend. And so the notion of Six Degrees of Separation evolved.

Probably the best-known experiment to support the notion of Six Degrees of Separation was conducted by an American researcher by the name of Stanley Milgram in 1967. He set out to see how many connections it would take to get a parcel from one randomly selected person to another in the US. He sent packages to a number of people in cities in the Midwest states, usually Wichita or Omaha, with the name of another randomly selected person in Boston on the East Coast. If, by chance, they knew that person in Boston then they were instructed to send the parcel directly to them. However, if they did not know them, then they should try to think of someone who might possibly know of this person. They should then send the parcel to them, with instructions to forward it on, and so the process was repeated. At the same time, each recipient sent a postcard to the researchers in Harvard so that they could keep track of the progress of the package. A log was kept and included in the parcel so that when it eventually arrived in Boston, the researchers could discover just how many people were involved in the chain from the Midwest to the East Coast.

Some parcels never made it to Boston. Others took as few as two connections while some took as many as nine or ten. Of the packages that did arrive, the average number of 'hops' on their route to Boston was between five and six, thus giving some credibility to the notion of Six Degrees of Separation.

It should be noted, however, that there are many critics of Milgram's experiment.

Whether there is any validity to the rule or not, there can be no doubt that building your network from the inside out is not as hard as it might first appear. After all, the people in your current network should be strong allies and supporters of yours – they should be eager and happy to help you. You should therefore think about the people that they might be connected to and specifically, how these individuals may be able to help you.

As you consider where to start, you should go back to your network audit and consider the Desired Number column of your audit; where do you need to focus first? Is it the internal, external or personal network that needs the most attention? Start on one at a time and write a list of people in your network who may be able to connect you with people in their networks who might be helpful to you.

You should build up a comprehensive list of people to talk to in this way, but be careful not to add just anyone to your list. There are a few common traps that you need to be aware of when you are thinking about who to connect with:

Don't just consider your everyday contacts: If you don't consider people beyond your daily interactions, your network will be too narrow and too focused in the here and now.

Actively look to include different people in your network: The last thing you want is a network of 'clones', or people with similar personality types or from similar backgrounds. You need to avoid groupthink in your network so ensure you include some people who will act as catalysts to challenge you and your thinking.

Don't discount competitors: You can gain valuable insights from competitors and suppliers, particularly those who have left your competitor organisations and moved on. They will have insights into your own business that you might never obtain from anywhere else.

Think broadly about your other external connections: Suppliers, customers, advisors, press and media, accountants, consultants, lawyers, government regulators or trade groups are all potential sources of contacts so do make sure you include them on your list.

It can be quite a daunting prospect as you first discover that your network needs work and then just how much work you are facing to get it to where it needs to be, but don't be disheartened. Establishing the network is always the toughest part; once it is up and running things get considerably easier.

Building from the outside in

By now you should have a long list of people to connect with in each of your personal, internal and external networks. These people have been identified through your current network and you are eager to get going. But before you do, it is worth stopping to reflect on whether there are people, areas or sectors that you would really like to target and connect with that may not emerge from your current list. In this case you have to consider approaching things from the opposite end of the connection.

CASE STUDY

Simon worked for the same organisation in the UK for fifteen years, running one of the divisions of the business and spending a lot of time overseas. He had spent many of his formative years in Africa but he did not want to return there. He enjoyed running his team around the world, the world of fast-moving consumer goods (FMCG), and working for this business where his career had progressed very well indeed.

Simon had a very well-developed internal network yet he had not invested much time in networking externally. Although he was known by his competitors, he only knew his counterparts in other organisations by name or reputation.

When a new CEO arrived at Simon's organisation, one of the first things that the new CEO did was to restructure the business. Simon found himself a casualty of the reorganisation and after fifteen years, needed to look for another role. It was a real shock for him, not least because he had never had to look for a new job.

Simon recognised that he did not have a good industry network and that this was an area that he needed to invest in, particularly because he wanted to continue in the sector. He identified four large organisations in the same area of FMCG that he had worked in previously, all of which he thought would have the sort of role that he would find challenging, rewarding and fulfilling. Simon's problem was that he didn't know anyone in any of these organisations. So he started asking questions of his current network – both former colleagues and suppliers to his previous business as well as other outside advisors such as his coach and a number of headhunters that he had used previously. Before long, he had not one name but several in each of the four organisations and personal introductions to three senior executives in two of his target businesses.

Within the space of three months, Simon had two job offers to consider as well as a commitment from a third person to keep Simon in mind for an opportunity that would arise as a result of a restructure taking place later in the year. In the end, Simon opted for one of the job offers that took him to a role in Asia - he has not looked back.

This is a classic case of building a network from the outside in. Simon was very clear about the organisations that he wanted to connect with and why. Once he had identified a small number of organisations, he worked back from there – who did he know who might know someone in each of them? Would they be prepared to introduce him? How should he position the introduction? He had a very clear strategy and was able to think creatively about how to implement it.

So when you are reviewing your audit and making plans to work inside to out, you also need to think about whether there are people, organisations or sectors that would be very useful to connect with, outside to in. If you identify a person or an organisation, it is then a case of thinking about who you know at the moment who might be able to connect you directly with them or, using the Six Degrees of Separation principle, whether they might know someone who might know someone who knows your target person or organisation. It may sound slightly complicated but, rest assured, it is much simpler in practice.

SUMMARY

Let's consider where you have got to so far:

▶ You have carried out a comprehensive audit of your current network. You have classified all of your contacts into personal, internal and external networks and you have prioritised each of them into one of three categories so that you connect with them monthly, quarterly or twice annually.

▶ You have evaluated how much time you spend networking currently and where you could add some networking activity.

▶ You have considered your Desired Number network and have identified the gaps that exist between your current and desired numbers.

▶ You have listed a number of people to connect with that will help you build your networks so that you get to your desired network numbers. This list has been compiled working on an inside out and an outside in basis where you have identified target people and organisations that you would like to have in your network.

You have completed all of the planning stages – it's time to get going.

Establish, Grow and Maintain

KEY POINTS

▶ Think about how you are communicating with your network and decide whether it should be face-to-face, phone, email, text or through social media channels.

▶ Always be prepared to reciprocate and offer something to your contacts.

▶ Create value for your network. Try to understand what might be of interest to your contacts and find things to fuel those interests.

▶ Make sure your network is fluid and review who is in it occasionally – people will and should be joining it and leaving it continuously.

▶ Learn to view networking as part of the way you work, not an onerous, additional activity.

In the first two chapters we have considered the purpose of networking and how to go about focusing where you need to build your networks and how to extend your reach of contacts. Now we will look at how to establish and develop relationships with your contacts.

One challenge that people are always concerned about is that of seeming to use people for personal gain. We are often asked: 'In building my network, aren't I just using people?' The honest answer is that sometimes, yes, you *are* using people, but if you are networking properly, that should not feel like the case.

You need to establish your network before you need it, not when you need it. If you take the latter course, then you may well feel that you are just using people because you have a greater and immediate need to benefit from a relationship with them. Your objectives will also become transparent to the people you are hoping to enlist support from, which puts them on the back foot at once. That's not to say that it is impossible to establish a great network when you need it most – we just saw with Simon's case study that it can be done – just that it may be more difficult. If you haven't already got a great network then start developing it now – you never know when you will need it and like any other investment, the returns pay back in the future, not immediately.

This chapter relates to some of the unwritten rules of networking: how to build trust in your network; how to create value for those in your network; and how to manage and maintain your network.

In the previous chapter we looked briefly at the three roles that you can play when networking: Giver, Taker and Connector (see pages 53–54).

There is no doubt that if you want to build your network quickly, the more Connectors you know, the better. Connectors will have well-developed and varied networks, which will be very diverse.

They are continually thinking about who will be helpful to whom and trying to put these people together. Their motives are selfless – they trust that in doing something helpful this will be reciprocated at some point in the future. We encourage everyone to think as Connectors do – it is enormously fulfilling and plays into some of our underlying emotional needs.

CASE STUDY

Rebecca had been a successful Human Resources Director for a large brewer in the Midlands. Wanting a change of career, she joined one of the UK's best known firms of headhunters. It was a very different role for her but because of her background she was asked to join the group that looked after searches in the sector of fast-moving consumer goods (FMCG) and also the specialist area of HR Directors.

Rebecca had spent most of her career helping people – she was a friendly, bright individual with a gregarious personality, so making new friends was not hard. She was very supportive of colleagues when working in her previous organisation and had taken the time to keep in touch with people who had moved on from the business; she'd also made sure to network with fellow HR Directors across a wide range of industries.

On arriving at the headhunting firm she was already very well networked and, unsurprisingly, it did not take her long to establish a great reputation. She was always very happy to meet people who were looking for new roles, or who were just seeking career advice, even though they may not have been able to support her in achieving her work objectives straight away. She was happy to put them in touch with others and to offer advice, even though this meant spending significant amounts of time away from completing her assignments.

Rebecca was a Connector. It was a role that she fulfilled naturally and in many respects because it fitted with her own extroverted personality. She was genuinely curious about people and their motivations and she wanted to help those that she met – never considering the quid pro quo. She trusted those people to return the favour as and when they were able, not that this was a condition of her meeting them. It never actually mattered to Rebecca if others did not reciprocate – the feeling of having done something good was sufficient.

It was therefore no surprise that when Rebecca chose to leave the headhunters to set up her own small boutique business, it flourished from day one. She rarely had to ask for favours as there was a queue of people who had benefitted from her advice and wisdom over the years who wanted to help her. Finding new work was never a problem – finding the resource to deliver it was Rebecca's new bottleneck. She did not stop meeting and connecting people; this was part of who she was and how she worked. Consequently, she was always in demand.

Being a Connector isn't for everyone. Some don't have the appropriate personality, others don't have the inclination or cannot think in the right way to make the connections really work. So if you don't feel that you are able to be a Connector, don't worry, just look out for those who are and ensure you invite them into your network – they will be the people offering to help or introduce you to people unprompted, seeing where mutual benefit may exist for you and others in their network.

Communicating with your network

In many respects, in getting to this point you have really done all of the hard work in establishing your purpose, identifying and prioritising your contacts, and recognising the different roles you will be playing within your network. So how do you now engage? What sort of conversation do you need to have? Is it a conversation at all; can't you hide behind an email instead?

Only you will be able to make that judgement, but to help you decide, you should think about a hierarchy of communications for your network:

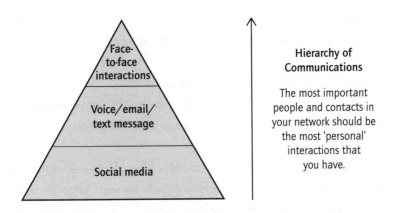

It may appear to be common sense, but you want to have the most personal interactions with the most important people in your network – at least to begin with. We will talk about how you maintain your network later on (see pages 80–88) but for now, the first impressions you make are going to be the most important, so you need to ensure that you present the best front possible, from appearance to manners, to make a great impression.

You should therefore try to meet your priority one contacts in person for the first time if you can. Emails and phone calls are easy to ignore, but once you are in front of someone it is very hard for them to disregard you.

Getting to this point can be a challenge in itself, although it may depend on how or who made the connection. If someone has referred you to an individual, always ask if it is all right to mention the mutual contact – you are much more likely to get time in someone's diary if you have been introduced by someone they already know. They may even take time to ask for a brief reference from the introducer, which is always useful and may lead to a much more fruitful discussion. But be careful – don't name drop without permission. Saying, 'James Kerr is a dear friend whom I have known for years' could backfire on you very badly if you met him a few years ago and only bumped into him again at a work event recently. A quick call with James will verify the fact that you hardly know him at all and will undermine your reputation and integrity.

Introductions nowadays are more often than not done by email. How you phrase these first emails is every bit as important as how you present yourself in the meeting itself. Assuming you did in fact know James Kerr and he introduced you to someone called Julie Ringer, consider the two introductory emails opposite:

Hi Julie,

I'm a friend of James Kerr and he said that it would be great if we could meet up sometime. Let me know when suits you.

Regards,

John

Or:

Dear Julie,

Please forgive this email out of the blue, but I was talking to a mutual friend recently, James Kerr.

James and I were colleagues at Axon plc a number of years ago. He mentioned that it might be worthwhile us getting together to discuss a project that I'm currently working on which may be of interest to you as it is in a similar field to your own area of work.

I'll ask my assistant to drop you a note to see if we can find a mutually convenient time and date to catch up soon and will look forward to meeting you in person soon – James speaks very highly of you!

With kind regards,

John

The information in the two emails is predominantly the same. They both talk about James Kerr as the common denominator and they both talk about meeting up soon. Which one do you think is going to lead to a meeting?

Of course, both may, but there is a greater likelihood that the second email will have a better success rate than the first. The first contains no context other than James is a mutual friend and that he suggested that a meeting might be a good idea. But it relies on Julie coming back to John with a time and date – without knowing what the meeting is about it's a very easy email to ignore.

The second email has a very different tone to it. It is slightly apologetic, to try to ingratiate the sender to Julie in the first place. It also provides more context as to how John and James know each other, which is helpful to Julie. But there are two more important aspects to it that give it a much higher probability of success.

Firstly, there is the offer that if Julie and John meet, Julie might get something out of the meeting as well – the point about the project being in a similar area to the work that Julie is doing is the key. There may be an exchange of information that could provide Julie with some learning. That is a very compelling reason to meet. Secondly, John is taking on the responsibility to arrange the meeting (or his assistant is). This is also key – it is easy for Julie to ignore the first email if she doesn't want to meet John, but in the second case, she is going to have to reply to John if she wants to avoid follow-up emails from his assistant. That simple act of her having to take the initiative to decline may be enough to get a meeting arranged. Simple points, but enormously effective.

Remember you cannot meet everyone face-to-face – at least not to begin with. You should make sure that you regularly prioritise your network to suit your current circumstances and objectives, whether you're looking for a new job opportunity or have a challenging project to deliver in your current role. Once you have figured out where to focus your efforts first, you should think about how best to phase your approaches. Of course, those on your priority one list are important, but you should not exclude making contact with some of your other network targets –for some a simple email or phone call may be enough to engage them and bring you into their consciousness.

Some simple phasing of your approaches will ensure that your diary management doesn't become too onerous. Remember your schedule of networking; you have roughly 112 hours a week available to fit in some networking and plan accordingly. Don't try to connect with twenty people in your list of priority one connections if you only have a spare hour a week to meet them. Knowing how challenging diaries are in the modern world, you run the risk of saying you will only be able to meet them in two months' time, which isn't impressive. Make sure you can offer time for a meeting within the next three to four weeks at the most, ideally sooner than that so the meeting remains in the front of their mind.

Now that you have finally arranged to meet, it's time to get to know your new acquaintance. There are three things to keep in mind:

1. First impressions really, really matter.

2. Do some research to find areas of mutual interest.

3. Find something to offer that may be of value to them.

We will talk about personal branding in the next chapter, but you cannot overestimate the importance of making a good first impression and the scary thing is, you probably only have a matter of seconds to do so. Humans have a fantastic decision-making facility that is capable of making snap decisions – it is called the adaptive unconscious.

Psychologist Timothy Wilson describes the adaptive unconscious as being the 'mental processes that are inaccessible to consciousness but that influence judgments, feelings or behaviour'. He continues, 'a lot of the interesting stuff about the human mind – judgments, feelings, motives – occurs outside of awareness for reasons of efficiency, and not because of repression . . . the adaptive unconscious has five defining features: it is non-conscious, fast, unintentional, uncontrollable, and effortless.'

In other words, it is what happens when you make instinctive judgements – whether you like how someone looks or not; whether you trust someone or whether you feel confident in what they might have to offer. The adaptive unconscious has a massive influence on how impactful your first impression will be. You cannot and must not underestimate the importance to you of how you come across when you first meet someone in setting the tone for a new relationship.

The second point is equally important. You need to find a hook for your conversation – simply talking about the weather, your holidays or the fact that your partner is a dance teacher is not good enough – these are the sorts of conversations you have with your taxi driver. You have to bring some value to the conversation and, ideally, you need to see if you can find some common ground or areas where you feel there might be some mutual interest.

It is worth spending time doing some research into the person that you are about to meet for the first time. If you have been introduced to them by a friend or colleague, ask them for some insights or information – what are their interests and hobbies; what sort of character are they; what are their likes and dislikes? The list is endless and, again, you have to make the judgement of what information to use and how best to use it. It may be slightly scary for someone if you launch into a detailed description of their career to date as your opening line:

> 'I understand you spent seven and a half years at a big accountancy firm before joining Company Z to be financial controller and that you only had a couple of years there before joining Company Y....'

It would be much more appropriate to say something along the lines of:

> 'I wonder – in your time at Company Z did you ever come across John Smith?'

The latter approach shows that you know something about them and that you also have a mutual connection to a company where they worked – whether they do or do not know John Smith is irrelevant – they will feel connected to you because of the acquaintance, however tenuous.

It will be more valuable, however, if you can find an area of mutual interest by demonstrating that you are curious about them and what they have achieved and this plays into the final point. You should always offer something in return for them giving up their time to meet you. It could be an introduction to someone or simply the name of a good book; the offer itself will demonstrate that you have valued the meeting and that you are willing to reciprocate to provide some mutual benefit. No one likes a taker who never offers anything in return.

One golden rule for your first meeting is to avoid self-promotion and talking about yourself; instead ask lots of questions about the person you are meeting – generally people like talking about themselves and feel good if you are taking a genuine interest in them. Remember though, this should not feel like an interrogation, but an authentic desire to get to know the person more intimately.

CASE STUDY

Bob was appointed to a new important role in a large, international business. He wanted to make an impression with his team and his new bosses, so he set about networking in earnest. He had a large agenda and his bosses had very material expectations of him – something they made sure that he appreciated in a forthright, if not assertive way.

Bob spent a great deal of time managing upwards. He emphasised the importance of the task at hand to his (large) team and at the same time, he was at pains to demonstrate to the team that he had the ear of the CEO and his fellow executives.

The more pressure that came on Bob and his team, the more he spent time managing upwards. He would have breakfasts with the CEO, drinks with the CFO and dinner with other senior executives, making the point to them that he was doing a great job and that he was responsible for the pace at which progress was being made.

What he failed to do was to create any followership with his team as he virtually ignored them, other than telling his team members about his meetings with all of those that he reported to. While his team did all the work, Bob was networking to further his own aims.

Two years into the role, Bob's team had delivered everything that had been asked of them, but Bob's reputation was all but destroyed. He had spent so much time networking up and outwards that eventually his bosses saw through him. His team received many accolades for what they had achieved and Bob was asked to leave. He had failed to acknowledge his team or to create any loyalty, and he had sought only to help himself. In the end, he had been found out.

This is an example of doing all the wrong things. Bob never offered anything to the people he was networking with, either those above him or those outside his own organisation. He worked to his own agenda, engaging in self-promotion at every opportunity. None of his team had a good thing to say about him because he took no interest in them – yes, he was civil and relatively engaging, but everyone could see that it was all about Bob. He rarely asked his team about them and their interests or challenges, rather he told them about his latest conversation with the CEO. It was extraordinarily wearisome.

Another key skill that is useful when first meeting new contacts is that of questioning. It can help you establish some common ground for further discussion, as well as demonstrating an interest in the other person. Simple things work well. If possible, avoid closed questions – ones that are going to elicit a yes or no answer – as that runs the risk of closing down the conversation and you have to begin all over again.

Instead try to ask open questions – questions that begin with what, when, where, how or why. Do be careful of asking a steady stream of questions, however – it can start to feel a bit like being interviewed by the Spanish Inquisition, which isn't very comfortable.

Once you have found the common ground that you are looking for, you should be off and running. Don't be put off if you cannot find anything in common – it's not a disaster. Instead, think about what has been in the news recently, and ask for the other person's opinions or perspectives.

Following up

You have met your contact; you have had a great conversation; you have explored a number of different avenues and there has been some mutual benefit to the meeting – they are firmly in your network. Now what?

Following up or, more correctly, not following up is where many people fall down in networking. They have an interesting meeting and commit to staying in touch but then squander that first positive meeting by failing to do so. You should reinforce that commitment by following up immediately. A brief email or text is more than adequate and it should highlight any promises that you have made to each other – something along the lines of the following should do:

Dear Helen,

Many thanks for your time yesterday. It was great to meet you and I'll be thanking Andy for the introduction to you when I see him in a couple of weeks' time.

You very kindly offered to introduce me to your
Technical Director, given our common areas of interest
so I look forward to hearing from them in due course.
Additionally, I'll send over the recent research document
that I mentioned to you during our conversation.

It would be great to keep in touch – perhaps I can
call you in two or three months' time once you have
completed your budgeting process.

Thanks again for your time and help.

With kind regards,

Jim

The key points in the above message are firstly, you are reminding Helen of the common connection who introduced you in the first place; you gently remind her of what she had offered (an introduction to her Technical Director) as well as your reciprocal offer (the research document) and finally you promise to maintain contact. You will note that the request to keep in touch is phrased as a statement rather than as a question – again, it places the onus on Helen to act if she doesn't want to maintain contact, and it becomes your responsibility to follow up with her in due course.

Don't feel that you should confine your follow-ups to regular intervals. With a network around 150 to 200 strong, you have an obligation to create some value for these people and to show an interest in them. If you see or hear of something that might be of value to them, don't wait until it is time to get in touch, do so immediately.

In the modern age there is so much information about people on the internet that it isn't difficult to find out what those in your network are up to. Some of your contacts may write blogs, so if you read something that is interesting, comment on it. Many people have LinkedIn profiles (the key business networking site; you should be connected to all your contacts on it), so if they update their profile, or use a new profile picture then make a comment or drop them an email through the system. You might even like to set up Google Alerts for the people in your network so that if they appear in the news or press, you will receive a notification. That is then your prompt to drop a note of congratulations if they have moved into a new job or achieved something notable. It is also worth scanning the business headlines for articles or news relating to the organisations in which people in your network work. It's easy to drop them a note saying something like: 'I noticed that your organisation was in the news recently – the expansion sounds like a really interesting investment'. It is the ideal excuse to connect with your network on something that is relevant to them.

We will look at other social media channels and how to use them most effectively in Chapter 7, but, for now, think about how you can use them to ensure that your network knows that you have them at the front of your mind – after all, it is enormously flattering and they will appreciate your attention.

Creating value in your network

Along with reciprocity, creating value in your network is one of the golden rules of networking. The question is what value do you bring to your network? You have a certain amount of knowledge and contacts, but who is to say that this is of value to others?

When thinking about what may be of value to someone else, you have to put yourself in their shoes. Imagine what sort of challenges might be keeping them awake at night, who they might derive some benefit from having a conversation with, or what trends and information might be useful to them. If you can work that out, then it is simply a question of matching it to what you know or who you know.

With this in mind, think about all the different people with whom your opposite number might be involved. What do you know about their customers and suppliers and what is happening in their world? What are the trends and influences in that particular sector? What about their competitors – what is going on with them? How about the advisors to your counterparty's business – is anything happening in that environment? What about the different geographies that they work in – is anything happening there that may be of interest to them? Are they likely to be affected by any regulatory issues or new legislation? How are they being viewed in the media – are there any relevant news stories related to them? What about their former colleagues or organisations where they have worked previously?

When you consider all aspects of another person's world, it would be very surprising if you can't find out something that is relevant to them, even in a small way, and even if they have already heard about it, it demonstrates to them that you have them in mind.

Creating value is about sharing, not hoarding; being creative rather than narrow-minded; and being open rather than closed. It does require some trust, but offering things and being generous is more likely to lead to benefits in the long term than not.

CASE STUDY

Anita is a well-known headhunter in London. Although she has a great reputation in the industry and rarely has to compete for work, even at the most senior levels in organisations, she is always alive to the possibility of creating value for the people she knows and appreciates the most.

She and her research team spend time scanning a variety of publications to understand what the trends are for senior leaders, what academics are researching or what may be happening at a macro level in the economy. When she finds something interesting, she makes the point of sharing that with the people that she feels may appreciate and value it. Not everyone receives the information from Anita, just the people for whom she thinks it is most relevant. It is a targeted approach and it works extremely well for her as it demonstrates the worth that she brings to her network. Her network reciprocates by calling her when they need her to find people for their various organisations. It is a win-win situation.

Acting as a Connector is the simplest and most effective way of creating value for your network, so you should always keep this in mind. Creating value is all about finding common interests and building on them through people, information or knowledge so that all parties benefit. Connectors are highly valued, because of their natural ability to do all this – they are generous and skilled at thinking laterally about how to create value through connections and contacts. So, what makes a great Connector?

You are interested: You have to show an interest in people and their businesses: what drives them; what they have done in the past; what they intend to do in the future; how they have got to where they are today; where they have worked and who they have worked with as colleagues, customers, suppliers and advisors.

You are curious: You have to be actively curious to discover new information and you have to be prepared to enquire on a range of different subjects. Career, ambitions, skills, strengths, development areas, interests, background and so on are all areas that might give you clues as to where you may find someone to connect this person to or an area of common interest.

You are well connected: Connectors have a well-developed and well-maintained network themselves. They have invested time in building credit within their networks so that when they ask something of their network, their request is rarely refused. Connectors network naturally and are happy to include a wide variety of people in their network. They see breadth as a real strength in their network rather than a limitation.

You have a sense of obligation: Connectors really understand the unwritten rules of networking. Their emphasis is always on creating value; on ensuring that there is reciprocity and mutual benefit when networking and this comes from their sense that they have to be Givers first and foremost. They set out to earn credit in their network before asking for favours in return. When they do take from their network they are always seeking opportunities for payback as soon as a possible.

You offer up first: You are the first to offer something during the course of a conversation. Pre-emptive offers are always greatly appreciated and it places an implicit onus on the corresponding person to offer something in return.

You are creative: This is the key skill of an effective Connector. You are able to join the dots and think about how you can effect an introduction and to whom. Often these opportunities emerge from thinking laterally and considering the extent of your network and how there might even be unorthodox matches that may create unexpected value for both parties. You have a bank of past conversations that is continually matched to your current conversations to ensure that you remain alive to opportunities to connect people.

Ongoing maintenance

Having established your network, maintaining it should be relatively straightforward. It's all about getting into the rhythm of networking and managing your diary. There is a wealth of Customer Relationship Management (CRM) tools available to help manage contacts, yet here we are talking about something incredibly personal. Your network is relevant to you and you alone; you have built and grown your network with a clear purpose. Everyone in your network is there because they have a specific role to play, whether it is to help you achieve your objectives; to help you grow and develop your career or to learn new things – everything relates back to you. So you need to maintain this network and keep it alive by nurturing it.

The key challenge therefore is to interact with the people in your network on a regular basis. During the course of the prioritising process, you will have determined how often that might be, but don't be put off by the size and scale of the challenge. Keeping in touch with 150 people in your network during the course of the year can appear daunting, particularly if you have a lot of people in your priority one list, but if you approach it in the right way, it should be perfectly manageable.

One thing to recognise is that – as we've said before – you don't always have to contact and connect with people in your network face-to-face. In fact, if you did you would have little time to do anything else all year. So as well as prioritising how frequently to contact the people in your network, you need to work out the best way to contact and communicate with them – whether it is in person (the most important), by email or phone or through another medium, such as one of the social media channels (the least important). Having said that, social media can be an incredibly useful tool to help maintain relationships in your network so you need to manage it appropriately – there is more on this in Chapter 7. So what do you say? Again, if you can, it's about creating some value but here are a few pointers that summarise what we've said so far:

1. Keep an eye out for interesting information to share.

2. Act as a Connector – look for common interests and objectives in your network.

3. Be human – send a quick message of congratulations, condolences or thanks when you see the opportunity to do so. A handwritten note is particularly impactful in the era of email and text.

4. Use all of your interactions to consolidate your relationship – if your intent is to have your counterparty in your network for the long term, try to solidify your relationship at every opportunity.

5. Be open – you will undoubtedly be caught out if you don't disclose relevant information to your network when you

have the opportunity to do so. Don't get caught out trying to be clever as it will always come back to bite you.

6. Avoid being competitive – particularly within your internal network. You may find yourself competing for roles or recognition. The bigger person steps back from this and always focuses on what is right for the business, putting personal ambition aside.

But back to the challenge of making networking intuitive and part of the way you work. For those who like structure, a well thought out spreadsheet with a list of names and contact details can be an invaluable tool and many have built and maintained excellent networks in this way. Some may be lucky enough to have a great PA who helps them manage their cycle of meetings and calls. For others, it may be a slightly random and ad hoc process, which isn't ideal because the probability of missing people out becomes far greater, meaning you run the risk of missing an opportunity.

This issue is what led to the idea of our app, BizPrompt, essentially a CRM system for individuals, designed to hold all the information on your network, including your priorities, and prompting you when to contact each person. The final section of the book provides you with detailed instructions on how to use the app. Tools such as this should help you incorporate maintaining your network into your everyday routine, so it doesn't feel like it requires additional effort on your part.

Networks are dynamic

Although you may have spent many hours building what you perceive is the perfect network, you cannot afford to rest on your laurels. You have to remain alive to the opportunity to add to your network on a daily basis . . . and as you add to your network, so you must delete from it as well. Remember, there is a limit to the number of people that you can maintain a meaningful relationship with so if you continually add, something or someone will suffer whether you like it or not.

Modern business is in a constant state of change and, with advances in technology, the pace of change has accelerated dramatically over the last twenty-five years. As your circumstances change, your career evolves and your interests develop, so must your network. What may have been relevant and interesting to you ten years ago may not be so now, and so your network needs to evolve to match those changes.

In the previous chapter we read about David, who had decided to leave corporate life and, instead, set up his own consultancy. We saw how he had developed his network in a very short period of time and how investing time in developing his network had paid dividends in growing his business.

Fifteen years on and David remains in the same business, but we caught up with him while researching this book to find out how he managed his network now. This is what he told us:

'I thought that my consultancy offering would be sufficiently compelling to have people knocking at my door and I wouldn't have to worry about finding work. This was not the case and it was a stark lesson to me. I realised very quickly that I had to go out to find business, particularly because what I was trying to sell relied on building great relationships, my clients trusting me and having me front of mind when the need arose. Selling

was all about managing my relationships and although I had a great reputation in the market place for my particular area of consultancy, it has only really been in the last two or three years that I have been receiving calls asking me to do work – some fifteen years after I initially set up my business. I never thought it would take me that long.

What I have discovered, however, is that my network has changed enormously over the years. It is probably the same size (around 200 people), but there has been a great deal of coming and going. I have lost touch with some clients that I was lucky enough to work with in the early days and I have started working with new clients who I have met, who have been referred to me or who have heard of me. Occasionally I get calls from people that I worked with over seven or eight years ago, asking me to do work for them, despite not having kept in touch regularly.

What's more, some of my own interests and areas where I'd like to develop personally have changed and evolved. I've dipped my toe in a number of different environments and as I've grown older, I've begun to focus more as these interests have narrowed, so my network has evolved to match that. What I pursued eight to ten years ago is very different to what is of interest to me now – and that is therefore reflected in the people that I connect with. And, with the advances in technology, you always have to be alive to what new developments are emerging so I try to keep abreast of thinking in this regard and make sure my external network remains current.

So with that in mind, I try to manage my network so that it doesn't get too unwieldy. At least every six months or so I sit down and go through my network to review exactly who should still be in it. It may sound harsh, but I only have a limited amount of time, so I cannot keep in touch with everyone regularly. I have learned how to prioritise my contacts and connections and also how to keep in touch with them. Some of the people that I haven't heard from or contacted in months, I drop from my network – that's not to say that I wouldn't invite them to a large event that we might be organising, but I don't reach out to them deliberately. If they contact me, that's different; I would always take their call, respond to their email or arrange to meet as you never know how you can help them or vice versa.

Managing my network is a really important part of how I work. I try to bring value to my network and ensure that if I'm reaching out to someone because I'd like to ask them for something, I always offer something in return that I hope will be of some value to them – after all, networking is all about mutual benefit not being selfish. As a personal rule, if I'm asking someone to introduce me to another person that they might know, I always ask if I can introduce them to anyone that I might know. And I always make sure I pay for the coffee.

So if I think about the people who are in my current network, compared to how it was fifteen years ago when I first set up my business, it has probably changed by around 60 to 70 per cent. Bizarrely, I can even think of a few people who have come and gone more than once!'

David's is a typical case of ensuring that his network remains fluid and dynamic. He is always open to the possibility that the next person he meets might be a critical member of his network and therefore if he adds someone, then another person has to drop off his radar. This may sound somewhat clinical and impersonal, but those who have been dropped from your network may still remain friends – all we are suggesting is that they are no longer actively managed and you do not reach out to them in a strictly professional/networking sense. You may still be in their networks, however, and they might reach out to you. If this is the case, then do as David does – always have a conversation because you never know what may emerge from it and you are building up credit.

There may also be a situation where you need to reach out to someone who was in your network some time ago, but who you haven't contacted for some time. This can sometimes feel very awkward and may lead to the other person thinking 'What does he/she want?' There are a few key pointers to try to make this easier and to diffuse any embarrassment:

1. **Acknowledge that time has passed.** It would be easy to send an email ignoring the fact that you haven't been in touch for ten years, but that would be inappropriate. The first thing to do is make a point of how much time has passed since you were last in touch. Making reference to something tangible that recognises the time elapsed, such as 'your children must have left university by now – they were still at school when we last spoke' is an easy way to break the ice. You should also offer up some information about what you have been up to since you were last in touch, be it work, personal or any other relevant point. Once you have done that you can move onto the next point.

2. **Be clear about why you are reconnecting.** As we have stressed in other chapters, it is vital that you are clear about the purpose of networking. You must be clear here too, and

specifically about why you are reconnecting after such a long time of radio silence. There is no point in reconnecting with someone simply for the sake of it – if this is your motive, by all means drop them a friendly note, but don't spend time trying to incorporate them into your network.

3. **Remember it is about mutual benefit.** With this in mind, think about some reciprocal value you might be able to offer, be it a connection or introduction or something else. You are starting off being a Taker but you must remember to be a Giver or Connector as well – that is one of the golden rules of networking.

Here is an example of a typical email, reconnecting with someone after a number of years have passed:

Dear Julie,

I trust you are well after all these years! Your name came up in a conversation with James Brocklebank at an event I was attending and I mentioned that you and I had worked together twelve years ago at Pinjarra plc – he was good enough to pass me your email address, hence this note. I find it quite terrifying how much time has passed since we last spoke – your children must all be grown up now as mine are.

James mentioned that you had recently being doing some interesting work with Queldon plc and using new technology to manage their inventory issues. This is a real problem we have at an organisation that I am doing some consulting with, so I wondered whether we might be able to get together to have a chat about what

*you are up to and how it is all going. Perhaps I can
get Jennie to see if she can find some times and dates to
catch up soon?*

*On another subject, James also mentioned that you had
a former colleague who was looking for some consulting
work – I'd be happy to have a conversation with him if
you would like to pass on my contact details. Just have
him drop me a note with his CV and we'll arrange to
have a chat.*

*I look forward to seeing you soon – I'm sure we'll have
lots to catch up on!*

With kind regards,

Simon

Simon has followed all three rules – acknowledging the break,
being clear about what he wants and offering to help Julie with
something. It should lead to a fruitful meeting, so you should
not be afraid of reconnecting with someone even though a
good deal of time has elapsed since you last were in touch.

SUMMARY

If you don't have a good network, building it can be very
daunting and time consuming – but that is not where it ends.
Maintaining your network is just as important as establishing
it in the first place. There are tools to help you manage the
maintenance of your network so that it doesn't become a drag,
so use them. Try to add value to your network by being curious,

generative and generous – remember, giving in the present will lead to payback in the future. Finally, make sure you always view your network as something that is dynamic and fluid. You will continually want to add to it as you meet new and interesting people but you must remember to subtract as well – don't lose sight of what the ideal size of your network should be to ensure that it doesn't become irrelevant or overwhelming.

You and Your Brand

KEY POINTS

▶ Be aware that first impressions really, really matter.

▶ Be clear about your elevator pitch; ensure it is concise and to the point.

▶ Be conscious that people have different personality types, and be prepared to adapt your approach.

When most of us think of branding, we tend to think of iconic names that we know, often relating to products, and let's face it, we all have our favourites for a variety of reasons. Some of us prefer Coca Cola to Pepsi, McDonald's to Burger King or Nike to Adidas. When we think of these brands, most of us are able to describe the logo or other key factors about the brand. Coca Cola cans and labels are red, Pepsi are blue and both logos are inherently different.

So how does this link to networking? The answer is that you have your own brand with its own set of brand values and identity – there is considerable correlation between company/product branding and personal branding. In a similar way to a company having a brand strategy that gives them a competitive edge, the same can be said about your personal brand. Your brand represents who you are, who you want to be and who people perceive you to be.

The foundation of any brand is the logo and in the context of your personal brand, this is the picture people have in their minds when they think of you. This can be based on the photo that accompanies your profile on social media websites, on your company website or the memory that people have of how you looked when they met you.

We know about the adaptive unconscious from the last chapter, and how people form their opinions of you in a split second. Whether these opinions are correct or not becomes irrelevant, it is quite simply human nature. We have all been in situations where we have looked at someone and formed an opinion about them; whether we think we will like them or not, if we will have things in common or even if we want to engage in conversation with them. What we must remember is that perception is reality. The image that we project to others will be the initial basis upon which their opinion of us will be based.

How people perceive you can be based upon many points – the way you dress, the way you carry yourself, your body language, handshake, eye contact and the way you communicate with people. It can even be about the devices you use: do you have a Nokia brick-like mobile from years ago or an Apple watch? Rightly or wrongly, people will sometimes make judgements about us based on what are seemingly irrelevant factors. Alongside a myriad of other factors, these are the things that we all too often forget as they become part of our everyday behaviours and lives. How we look and our accessories are every bit as important as our intellect and eloquence.

One physical form of your personal brand is your business cards. How do they look? Are they pristine because you keep them in a business card holder or a bit grubby, dog-eared and handed over with accompanying fluff due to having been kept in your pocket? Do they feel of high quality or do they look as if you had them produced in a DIY print store? What about your job title? Do you portray the image of someone who looks like the common perception of the typical person in your job role? Is your job title recognisable to those outside your organisation? We may be labouring the point here, but in some cultures, the exchange of business cards is a very important ritual and worth taking time to think about.

Jeff Bezos, CEO of Amazon, says 'Your brand is what people say about you when you're not in the room.' Their judgements won't just be based upon whether or not they like you, they will be based upon innumerable factors such as what they have read about you or pictures they have seen of you online, your posts on Twitter or Facebook, what others have said, their personal experiences of time spent with you or your written communication with them. The list is endless. As we mentioned in Chapter 1, a primary, basic human need is to be liked. We want people to like us, even those that we don't know or haven't yet met.

CASE STUDY

A financial services firm with a high profile hired a new CEO to replace the incumbent, who was retiring after thirty years with the organisation. Michael, the new CEO, was an American who had spent most of his career in Asia, working for one of the world's largest banks in a wide variety of roles. He was well suited to the job as the Board were eager to modernise the firm and bring it into the twenty-first century.

Based in a small regional town in the UK, the firm had a somewhat stuffy reputation and its retiring CEO was definitely old school. The offices were all private and large oak desks sat in the middle of each room for the executives and managers to work at. The boardroom and other main rooms had lovely oak panelling and a slightly musty smell as they weren't used that often. The outgoing CEO had ruled with a rod of iron and controlled almost everything, from stationery orders to major decisions on strategy – he even opened all of the mail first thing in the morning.

Michael, therefore, was always going to be quite a shock for the organisation and the organisation was going to be quite a shock for him. He was very bright, quite introverted and empathetic towards his staff, and this was his first appointment as CEO.

Michael's whole approach came under close scrutiny from the moment his appointment was announced. Everyone in the business tried to find out as much about him as they could before he started, via the internet, press cuttings and social media. When he eventually arrived for his first day, his every move was studied closely: people noticed the car that he was driving; where he parked it in the car park (the old CEO had a named space, but Michael parked in the first one that he came to); how he greeted the girls at the front desk (he stopped, said hello and asked them their names, and introduced himself rather than ignoring them as his predecessor did); what type of suit he was wearing; the make of his wristwatch – there was not a single detail that went unnoticed. Whether Michael was conscious of this was another matter altogether.

Before a week was up in his new role, he went into the room where the more junior PAs and secretaries worked to say hello and to introduce himself to them all. To his surprise and shock, one of the young women burst into tears and had to leave the room. He discovered later that the only time the previous CEO went into that room was to fire one of them and this time, the woman thought it was her because she was the first person he spoke to.

Michael reflected on that experience over the weekend and recalled when he, as a young graduate fresh out of university, had been at a dinner with the CEO of a large American bank and how he had felt then. He remembered his own anxiety and fears, particularly when the CEO asked him for his views on something, and he realised that he had become that person. Fundamentally, he had not changed, yet with the title 'CEO' on his business card his personal brand had changed and along with it, the expectations and perspective of all the people around him.

Your personal brand is represented by every element of who you are – from your values, beliefs, networks, friends and interests, to your career choice, the company you work for or own, to your manners, your communication style, your ability to build rapport with others and numerous other factors. Think about the following questions, which we will consider throughout this chapter:

- What are your opinions?

- How well do you communicate?

- How do you dress and how much importance do you place on your appearance?

- What impression does your online persona give to others?

Your personality traits tend to have a big impact on your personal brand. Do you portray a different image at work to the one you have in your personal life? If someone you work with described you to a stranger who didn't know you and someone you know in your personal life did the same, would they be describing the same person? That's not to say that it's wrong to be different at work; it can be dependent on your job role, the industry sector you work in, your level of seniority, your career aspirations and more. The important thing is to be aware of any changes in your behaviour in and out of the office and be consistent; so if you are socialising with colleagues or clients, maintain a professional conduct.

Whether you are an individual or a team player, a confident or shy person, a born communicator or quiet, a leader or a follower, you should strive to be consistent in the brand that you portray to others. We've all heard stories about office Christmas parties, when the seemingly quietest person in the company suddenly turns into the life and soul of the party after a few glasses of wine. Peers may well change their mind about them, they may have good conversations with them and interact with them like never before, only to find that the morning after they have retreated back into their shell. Consistency is key and this is as important at work as it is outside of it:

CASE STUDY

Danny ran the sales teams in a small family business. He wasn't a family member, but he had been with the organisation for many years and was in with the bricks. He was a very competitive individual – he had played both winter and summer team sports competitively and played other individual sports as well, such as golf and squash. It seemed like everything was a competition to him and he brought this to work.

Unfortunately, while providing a competitive edge was very helpful from a sales perspective, his team did not like the way he managed and led them. His character was unpleasant and aggressive to the point that many sometimes felt bullied by Danny, although he had never had anyone accuse him formally of this type of behaviour.

What may have saved him from a formal complaint was the fact that outside of the office, he was the life and soul of the party. He was generous and kind and everyone liked to socialise with him. He had a great sense of humour and engaged with everyone in a group in a very genuine and authentic way, which was totally at odds with how he behaved in the workplace. It was very confusing for his colleagues.

Danny's inconsistency was mystifying, and many of his friends and colleagues saw him as a Jekyll and Hyde character and wished that he could bring some of his social personality into work to enable him to become more human and less aggressive. His personal brand was very ambiguous and inconsistent and it did not serve him well at all.

While Danny was engaging and friendly outside of the office environment, clearly he was a different person when he was at work. Inconsistency is troubling for people as they cannot understand which person they are dealing with so do try to ensure your brand values and approach are consistent, predictable and reliable.

Now that we've considered the importance of your personal brand, let's look at some of the key things that can affect it and the way you are perceived by others. Some of these may seem obvious, but others are more subtle and definitely worth consideration.

First impressions count

Albert Mehrabian is a Professor Emeritus of Psychology at UCLA in the USA. He is best known for his work in the area of verbal and non-verbal messaging. In 1967 he undertook some research and published two papers that dealt with this particular issue. His summary was an equation for 'total likeability', which is:

$$\text{Total liking} = 55\% \text{ facial liking} + 38\% \text{ vocal liking} + 7\% \text{ verbal liking}$$

In other words, how you look and how you sound is incredibly important. It is commonly acknowledged that people make their judgement of you within one-tenth of a second of seeing you. As Mehrabian hypothesised, 93 per cent of that first impression will be based on visual and vocal impressions with the remaining 7 per cent based on the words you say. There can be a generation gap with this; older people will generally take longer to make their judgement due to slowing processing skills (not to mention having grown up in an era where technology was less prevalent) whereas the younger generation, encouraged by the digital world, may judge more quickly. Take new technology applications like Tinder, where your decision is taken purely on the basis of how someone looks. The choice of swiping left if you don't like the person or swiping right if you do, is based on a judgement made in seconds.

First impressions can make or break an opportunity to create new relationships and build existing ones. Creating a poor first impression can cause someone to decide not to get to know you or perhaps prevent them from making introductions that would be beneficial to you. First impressions last much longer and carry much more importance than we may think, and we may be limiting our own success by creating a bad one. Think about all the times you have said, 'Oh, she's being grumpy because she's having a bad day. She isn't usually like that.' We defend people when they behave outside our expectations because our first impression of that person has more weight in future communications than subsequent exchanges have.

You may have heard of the 'halo effect', a term coined by psychologist Edward Thorndike in reference to how a person is perceived by others. The halo effect works in both positive and negative directions (the 'horns effect'): if the observer likes one aspect of something, they will have a positive predisposition towards everything about it. If the observer dislikes one aspect of something, they will have a negative predisposition towards everything about it. So, what should we consider when thinking about the first impression we make?

Visual impressions play an instrumental role in networking, not least since you will usually be seen before you are heard.

Before you utter a word, people will start making judgements about you relating to various factors including appearance, approachability, professionalism, intelligence, values, confidence and success. We will cover more about this in Chapter 5 but here are some key factors to consider:

Appearance

Top of the list of visual judgements is your appearance. What does your appearance say about you? A polished appearance can create a positive impression as well as displaying professionalism and increasing your confidence. It is also important to consider what style of dress is appropriate for the environment you are in. For example, if you are a man going to a formal black-tie dinner, it is inappropriate to wear a lounge suit, even with a tie. If you are attending a business networking event, consider what type of event it is going to be, who will be attending and whether they are likely to be dressed formally or casually. If you arrive at an event dressed casually and everyone else is smartly dressed, you may feel awkward for standing out. Even if you are dressing casually then remember to be well presented – you don't always have to wear a suit to radiate professionalism.

The culture of an organisation will also tell you a great deal about how to dress; simply looking around will help you understand this better. It is important to try to match where possible to try to show that you are making an effort to fit in. Banks can be quite traditional – suits and ties (often the corporate tie) can be de rigueur, so showing up in jeans and a polo shirt isn't likely to be well received. On the other hand, that same outfit might be completely acceptable in a creative agency, where being free-spirited and unconventional is valued. It's tricky. Where possible, fitting with the accepted convention is going to serve you better, whether you're at an event or your place of work.

Dressing appropriately for both work and events will have a positive impact on your relationships with all of your networks. Even seemingly simple things such as an ironed shirt and well-polished shoes go a long way to creating the right impression. It was mentioned to us when starting out in our careers that we should dress for the position we wanted, not the one that we were in. Sage advice for many; however, be careful that you don't alienate yourself from your peers by taking this to the extreme.

Body language

Body language can speak more than words and it accounts for a bigger percentage of our communication skills – remember Mehrabian's equation; 55 per cent of total liking is accounted for by facial liking or the expressions on our face and our body language.

Body language complements verbal communication in social interaction and is where thoughts, intentions or feelings are expressed by physical behaviours, such as facial expressions, body posture, gestures, eye movement, touch and the use of space. Let's consider the most important considerations when it comes to body language.

Eye contact

'The eyes are the window to your soul' is a quote attributed to Shakespeare, although there is some doubt as to the truth that it was the Bard who first came up with the saying. In *Divine Weekes and Workes, Sixth Day* Guillaume Du Bartas said 'These lovely lamps, these windows of the soul.'

Whatever the source of the quote, eye contact is extremely important during communication. A person's eyes reveal much about what they are feeling or thinking. Eyes also reflect our sincerity, integrity and comfort when communicating with another person. This is why having good eye contact while engaging with others is one of the key indicators that the communication is going well.

Eye contact also demonstrates that you are a good listener, which is key to building a rapport with them. When you maintain eye contact with the person you are talking to, it indicates that you are focused and paying attention to what they are saying. Steady eye contact also shows an openness in communication and can help to build trust and respect.

On the other hand, sporadic eye contact and looking away could be interpreted by the other party as you not wanting to engage with them, or disliking them, which may, in turn, result in them projecting negative feelings towards you.

Eye contact is a key tool in creating a good first impression, so remember the following points:

- Connect with the person or people you are engaging with by tilting your head slightly to one side and looking directly at them. Giving them your full attention and showing you are listening will encourage them to share more with you.

- Remember it's not a 'stare out'. Ensure your eye contact is steady but not piercing; there is nothing worse than making someone feel uncomfortable by being stared at. Give the person three to five seconds of eye contact then briefly look away before focusing on them again.

- But equally don't let your eyes wander, which will make it seem as if you are not interested.

- When talking with a group of people, try to distribute your eye contact evenly among all parties. We are subconsciously driven to look at people with whom we feel we have the biggest connection and like the most and it can be very easy to end up focusing on one individual to the exclusion of others.

Facial expressions

Understanding facial expressions and their meaning plays a key role in the communication process, so pay attention when talking to people to make sure you are reading their smiles and frowns correctly. The interpretations that we assign to these facial expressions can vary greatly, so we must be careful when using them to prepare ourselves for the way in which they may be interpreted. We tend to annotate facial expressions differently based upon our background and experience and, as such, we can easily misunderstand the intent behind these nonverbal cues. Be aware of your facial expressions and control them according to the situation you are in. Smiling is fundamental to developing rapport and building trust in your relationships so do it and do it often. There are also some cultural nuances to consider here – we will touch on these later in the book but, for now, be conscious of the culture in which you are operating and the implications on how you appear to others.

Posture

Good posture should be natural and relaxed, not stiff and tense, so be aware of your stance and make sure it matches the words you are saying. Slouching or standing with your hands in your pockets can be interpreted as laziness and a 'don't care' attitude, whereas standing up straight will be seen as being attentive and interested.

A closed posture can give the impression of disinterest, dislike and detachment. Examples of closed posture include:

- Arms folded across the chest or abdomen
- Hands clasped in front of the body
- Crossed legs
- Clenched fists
- Hands clasped behind the back
- Slouching as if uninterested
- Fidgeting
- Swaying or rocking back and forth

On the other hand, an open posture indicates a friendly, positive and confident attitude:

- Head straight and chin raised
- Maintaining eye contact
- Leaning forward – although be aware of personal space
- Relaxed and open hands
- Showing the palms of the hands

Non-visual
Non-visual cues don't tend to feature as highly for many people when thinking about first impressions; however, they can still be just as important as visual ones.

Spatial awareness

Most people value their personal space and feel discomfort, anger, or anxiety when it is encroached upon. Proxemics, the study of measurable distances between people as they interact with one another, was introduced by Edward T. Hall in 1966. Based upon two phases, close and far, his recommendations for optimal distances for social interaction among acquaintances were 46 to 76cm (close) and 76 to 122cm (far).

You will probably have met someone in the past who, during a conversation with you, has virtually pinned you up against a wall or been so close to you that you could feel their every breath on your face. Changing the distance between you and the person you are communicating with can demonstrate very different messages depending upon circumstances. Moving closer towards someone can indicate a desire for interest, intimacy, anger or domination. Moving away from someone can indicate that you are not interested in what they are saying, you're not comfortable being in conversation with them or that they have encroached on your personal space.

Watch the person's body language carefully and if you feel they are uncomfortable with the distance between you then subtly adjust it by moving forward or back.

Speech

There are several points to be considered when looking at the importance of speech in the first impressions you make – accents, speed, volume, vocabulary, tone and intonation all play pivotal roles. Accents can be challenging. If you have a strong accent or you have a different first language, it can be difficult for people to understand you. It is of utmost import-ance to be aware of how you talk and make sure you are speaking as clearly as possible. Avoid using local dialect, which may not be understood by the person you are speaking to.

The speed at which you speak is also very significant. If you speak too quickly, people may not catch what you are saying. Alternatively, if you speak too slowly, people may become bored. In both of these scenarios, the chances are that the person you are speaking to will switch off and stop listening. Try to speak at a regular speed and watch out for signs that the person doesn't understand what you are saying such as lack of eye contact, raised eyebrows or tipping their head to one side demonstrating a non-verbal question. Pause for effect where applicable, just be careful it doesn't seem as if you've forgotten what you were going to say.

Volume is a more difficult judgement to make. Speaking too loudly will instantly alienate you from the person you are communicating with, just as much as speaking too quietly will. Try to adjust the pitch, tone and volume of your voice according to the environment you are in. If there is a lot of background noise then you may need to speak more loudly than you are accustomed to. Equally, if you are in a quiet environment, tone this down a little. Once again, watch for body language from the person you are communicating with for any indication you are not getting it right.

The vocabulary you use is also meaningful. We have no doubt all been in situations where the person we are communicating with uses words that we don't understand, so try to avoid industry-specific acronyms or jargon. On the other hand, if you know that the person will know what such terms mean, you can end up impressing them with the knowledge and expertise you have in your sector and industry. Do, however, be careful that you do know what you are talking about so you don't get caught out.

Finally, tone of voice and intonation are important. There is nothing worse than listening to someone who speaks in a monotone. It is one of the primary factors that results in the person you are speaking to switching off. Try to vary the tone of your voice – most of us do this naturally but, if you're not sure, ask a colleague or friend or better still, record yourself, play it back and work on making adjustments to your voice accordingly.

CASE STUDY

Shona worked in recruitment specialising in the electronics sector. Her job included spending time on-site with clients to gain a better understanding of how they operated and to get to know their culture. The role was varied and required a high degree of adaptability depending upon the environment she was in, and who she was dealing with at the company.

One particular client was going through extensive expansion and unusually, Shona had two meetings on two consecutive days at the client premises. The first meeting was with the chief executive to discuss a board position and the second with one of the factory supervisors regarding an operator role.

The day of the first meeting, given that she was going to meet the CEO of the company, Shona made sure she looked extra smart and wore a new suit. She felt confident as she drove to the meeting and was pleased that she had made more effort than usual with her appearance. The meeting went well and the conversation flowed. Shona made sure that she used management speak when talking to the CEO to ensure they were on a level playing field. They discussed the future growth strategy for the business and she felt comfortable that she had a good understanding of the type of candidate they were looking for.

The following day, for her meeting with the supervisor, Shona made the decision to dress slightly more casually. She decided that a suit would be overkill but still wanted to look smart so chose a shirt and skirt instead. She had new shoes that had fairly high heels but she thought they went well with her outfit. She arrived at the client premises and once again felt confident that she looked the part and was well prepared.

During the discussion with the supervisor, she asked similar questions to the ones she had the day before, but noticed that the supervisor was looking somewhat puzzled by some of the things she was asking. She realised that he hadn't understood some of her phrases, and quickly adapted her communication style to match the language that the supervisor was using. Having done so, the conversation flowed much more smoothly with no awkward pauses and she was able to glean the information required to be able to find the right candidate for the role.

The supervisor suggested that he gave her a tour of the shop floor, which she was eager to do; nothing made filling a job easier than actually seeing the environment and understanding the processes. What she hadn't realised was that in order to see the clean room, she was going to have to wear shoe covers, which proved somewhat problematic to put on over a pair of high heels and made it tricky to walk. As she was walking around the shop floor, she felt a little self-conscious as all the operatives were casually dressed and she felt that she stood out rather more than she would have liked.

Hindsight is a wonderful thing, she thought, wishing that she had worn more sensible shoes.

She was delighted, however, that once the tour came to an end, the supervisor gave her two roles to fill rather than just one and told her that she'd impressed him with her attention to detail in terms of gaining a full understanding of the job role and with the questions she had asked in order to do so.

In most respects Shona had done things correctly in terms of making sure that the language she used at the meetings with both parties matched their language, albeit after having to adjust it with the supervisor. She had ensured that her clothes were appropriate to the environment, but what she could have improved upon was thinking about the environment she was going to on the second day and making sure that she wore more sensible shoes. This may seem like a minor point, but she felt self-conscious during the factory tour, which impacted on her confidence levels.

This clearly demonstrates the importance of adaptability; it's essential that you temper the language and tone of your communication style and your appearance to suit the environment you are in and this is applicable to networking as it is to numerous other aspects of life. Nothing will impact more on your confidence levels than feeling uncomfortable for any reason so ensure that you give this sufficient thought and consideration.

Written communication
In the twenty-first century, communication increasingly takes place electronically, whether that is via emails, texts, messaging

apps or other online means. Written communication is one of the most challenging media to communicate in as it can often be hard to understand the context or meaning behind a message without any visual or audio cues: no tonality, body language, eye contact, in fact, no chemical interaction at all. To make matters more challenging, emails, texts and messages will be there forever, and can be copied and sent on to other people, so if you are writing something important to someone, do be conscious of its almost eternal lifespan.

The tone of written communication can vary enormously from one organisation to another. Some may be relatively informal and others may be verging on what could only be described as old-fashioned and overly formal. An important consideration for the younger generation is to avoid writing emails and other business communications in 'text speak'. What we mean by this is using abbreviations and words that could be incomprehensible to those from a different generation. Use the correct grammar and spell-check every communication before you send it. It's all too easy to send out an unprofessional and grammatically incorrect communication to someone with whom you are trying to engage. Consider the following two examples:

Hey James – gr8 to see you lst night at the event. Let's do coffee b4 too long. Andy

And:

Dear James

It was a pleasure to meet you at last night's networking event in the City. I do hope you returned home safely and weren't caught up in the interminable traffic that we seem to be cursed with currently.

I would very much like to continue our conversation about the intricacies of the technological advances that you are experiencing at present. I will ask our respective Executive Assistants to touch base and arrange a further meeting at our mutual convenience, sometime in the next three to four weeks.

With kind regards,

Yours sincerely,

Andy

Clearly the first email is too curt and 'text speak' in its layout, which may be fine if James and Andy are young professionals who regularly interact this way. The second could be considered overly formal in its look and feel. But for two non-executive directors of large public organisations, that too might be the perfect (and expected) way to communicate. You need to be aware of these subtle nuances and adapt your own written style to match the anticipated style of the recipient of your communiqué. If you are emailing outside your organisation to someone in your network who you don't know particularly well, or have perhaps only met a couple of times, always err on the side of caution. It's better to be overly formal rather than too familiar.

Don't be tempted to hide behind emails and use them as your primary communication source. Sometimes it can be much easier and you can build better relationships by simply picking up the phone and communicating verbally. Nothing builds rapport faster than getting to know people properly, whether that is by phone or face-to-face. It is a much quicker way of developing relationships and building trust.

What not to do

When trying to make a positive first impression, no matter how engaging your conversational skills are, there are several basic behaviours that are totally destructive and will demean every word that you say. These include:

- Not listening and appearing uninterested

- Looking around the room rather than maintaining regular eye contact

- Checking your watch

- Jangling change in your pocket or fidgeting

- Your phone ringing

- Appearing bored

- Being long-winded

- Complaining about things

- Being overly opinionated

- Being boastful

- Bad breath

Your behaviours must be in sync with your conversation to avoid running the risk of ruining the impression the person has of you. Consistency is key to your success both for your career and in terms of achieving your networking goals.

The elevator pitch

Your elevator pitch is essential when networking to ensure that you are well prepared and comfortable with introducing yourself to strangers, for example at events or when meeting a new client for the first time. What five words would you use to describe yourself? What five words would a stranger who had spent an hour talking to you use to describe you? The more you can distil the essence of your personality and your key strengths in the way that you present yourself, the more positive the impression that you'll leave. Your elevator pitch is an extension of this. The principle is that it is a pitch (originally for a film idea) that could be delivered in the space of an average elevator ride if you ever happened to find yourself in a lift with a Hollywood producer. Unlikely for most of us, we have to confess; however, the principle is equally applicable to networking.

The elevator pitch is often used in a sales and marketing context, but it's applicable to anyone who wants to make a fast and long-lasting impression on the people they meet. Think about a situation where you might be asked to tell someone a little about yourself, for example at a networking event. Could you do it in the space of an elevator ride? The key is to make it clear, succinct, easily understandable and consistent with your personal brand.

Your elevator pitch should be between thirty and sixty seconds long and should be delivered in an engaging way, with enthusiasm, and good pitch and tone in your voice. Don't overcomplicate it; it should be easy to understand so make sure you avoid industry-specific words and acronyms that mean nothing to those outside your sector. Try to restrict your key messages to three – it becomes easier for you to remember and, more importantly, it is easier for the other person to remember. It should also leave the person you are speaking to wanting to ask a question to find out more about you, and you should conclude it with your own question to the person you are speaking to in order to demonstrate your interest in finding out more about them.

An example of a good elevator pitch would be as follows:

> *Hello, my name is Stewart Crighton and I'm the Business Development Director of Malones. We're a full service digital agency and specialise in the hospitality sector working with companies such as Protraction plc. I've been with them for two years and my team has grown considerably in that time. What do you do?'*

In three short sentences, Stewart has given a lot of information, yet delivered it in a succinct way that doesn't take long to deliver and should hopefully pique the interest of who he is speaking to. There is nothing worse than asking someone what they do at a networking event and still be waiting two minutes later for an explanation that makes sense.

Something else to bear in mind when thinking about your elevator pitch is your job title. Remember that if you want to be easily understood and be on a par with your peers as we discussed earlier in the book, you need to make it as clear as possible to people you meet what it is that you do and at what level in the organisation you are. As the adage goes, KISS – Keep It Simple Stupid. There's no benefit to be had from overcomplicating things and putting extra hurdles in your way when meeting new people you hope to develop a relationship with.

CASE STUDY

Jonathan had done a fair bit of networking in his time and was pretty confident about attending events. He had eventually taken the plunge and decided to set up his own business doing web design. He was looking forward to the first event he was attending since establishing the company and was sure that his passion and enthusiasm would shine through.

He was pleased when he saw, from the delegate list that had been circulated prior to the event, that several people he was keen to meet with a view to developing a relationship with were going to be in attendance and wanted to make sure that he met as many as he could. He had spent considerable time designing his new logo and business cards and was really pleased with how they looked. He'd decided that rather than have a standard job title of Managing Director, he would go with something more quirky and memorable so had chosen the title 'Design Ninja'.

On arriving at the event, he bumped into various people he knew and had brief catch-ups with them all before he spied one of the people he was keen to meet. Putting on his most engaging smile, he approached the lady who fortunately had just left a group she'd been chatting to.

'Hello, my name is Jonathan Runcorn, I'm Design Ninja with Capture Creative, it's nice to meet you.'

The lady looked somewhat bemused, which caught him by surprise.

'Hi, good to meet you too, I'm Tracy Burlington, I'm the Digital Director for Momentum. So what exactly is it that you do? I understand from the name of the company that you're obviously in the creative sector but who on earth came up with such a ridiculous job title - you must have a very strange boss.'

The danger with trying to be different sometimes, is that you can end up alienating yourself or as happened to Jonathan, feeling embarrassed and slightly foolish that what you or your boss thought was a quirky job title can backfire. Jonathan was obviously keen to build rapport with Tracy, but he was immediately on the back foot after her comment about his boss having given him a ridiculous job title when in actual fact, that boss was him.

Another benefit of having a well-honed elevator pitch is that it can help you to overcome any nerves that you have about networking. To know and have learnt your pitch means that no matter what situation you find yourself in, you will always have something to say which will be informative.

When delivering your elevator pitch remember to be:

- Enthusiastic
- Concise
- Engaging
- Dynamic
- Interesting

You and your reputation

Perception is reality and nowhere is this more true than in your reputation. Is it what you want it to be? Your reputation can take years to build and milliseconds to ruin. Your persona as a credible, powerful, successful business person will open doors for you, so make sure that you do everything you can to enhance it at every opportunity. Your reputation needs to be good inside and outside your network.

Do people who know you describe you as the consummate professional who's always willing to help others? Do they say that you are friendly and outgoing? Do they say that you're enthusiastic and passionate? What would you want them to say about you? Is there synergy between what you want them to say and what they actually say?

And how about people who've never met you? What have they heard about you? What have they read about you online? Does your LinkedIn summary match who you truly are? Do your tweets portray the image that people have of you? Are your Facebook posts about what you did on Saturday night when you were out and about public for the world to see or only visible to your friends? We will look at this in more detail in Chapter 7.

Many people may not want to actually ask others what they think of them; however, these days, with many organisations using 360-degree feedback, even those who shy away from the answers are often put into the spotlight, whether they wish to be or not. Even if your company doesn't use 360-degree feedback, there are still ways you can find out: by asking colleagues and peers, by asking your network, by asking your clients and customers; the opportunities are endless. If you do ask others then it's important to ask them to be honest with you. There is little point in asking someone who is going to tell you what you want to hear. Tell them that you would really appreciate their opinion and ask if there is anything they think that you could improve upon.

Your reputation has the potential to open doors for you, so make sure that you do everything you can not to stand in your own way. If you have a good reputation, people will feel positive about introducing you to their network, will invite you to important meetings or events, and crucially, will want to spend time in your company.

Likewise, a bad reputation is likely to have a negative effect, closing doors to future opportunities. Samantha's tale is a salutary lesson:

CASE STUDY

Samantha was really looking forward to her holiday with three of her close friends. She really needed a break, having been working very hard on a project that had required very long hours. The chance to enjoy some sunshine, relax and switch off was just what she needed and being with her best friends would be an added bonus. Heading up a fairly sizeable team at work meant she was constantly asked for her opinion and advice, particularly as she was highly respected among her peers.

The holiday got off to a great start; the hotel they were staying in was lively and there were plenty of people around their own age to socialise with. There was a bar in the pool that was always busy and the girls spent quite a bit of time there chatting to fellow guests.

A couple of days into the holiday, they were at the bar speaking to a group of young men from London who were all good fun and there were plenty of laughs. They made a pact not to discuss which companies they worked for and what they did for a living; after all, this was a holiday and no one wanted to think about work. They had exchanged names, but that was as far as it went. One drink led to another and another, and so it continued for most of the afternoon. They were all being pretty raucous by this point and Samantha, with her outgoing and fun personality, was proving to be the life and soul of the party.

As the wine and conversation flowed, so did the stories. Samantha, not being at her most aware due to the number of drinks she had consumed and her enjoyment of being in the limelight, decided to tell the rest of the group about one of her clients and his extra-curricular activities. In the haze of several drinks, she mentioned the client's name and company while entertaining and sometimes shocking everyone with their somewhat colourful activities outside work. The group found it highly amusing and the more questions they asked, the more details Samantha shared with them.

A couple of days later, one of the girls picked up a UK newspaper in the hotel shop before breakfast and brought it down to the pool. Samantha made a quip about who would want to read a paper when they were on holiday, she certainly wouldn't!

A few minutes later, her friend exclaimed, 'This is a nightmare, I can't believe what I'm reading. I think you'd better take a look Samantha, this is unbelievable, you're not going to be happy.'

She passed the paper over to Samantha and to her utter horror, there, splashed across a full page in the newspaper was a photo of the client she'd been talking about a couple of days previously along with an article detailing all the extra-curricular activities he got up to in his spare time, citing Samantha as the source. She couldn't believe what she was reading. While it was true and factually correct, to have it splashed all over a national newspaper and have it linked to her name was nothing short of all her worst nightmares come true.

What subsequently ensued turned out to be the most disastrous scenario Samantha could have imagined. The managing director of her company called and told her in no uncertain terms that her employment contract was being terminated due to gross misconduct. She received calls from colleagues, family and friends, not to mention several very disgruntled clients, all of whom expressed their disbelief at her stupidity and indiscretion. What had been a fun and much looked forward to holiday had imploded. She had no job to return to and she had ruined her professional reputation.

To make matters worse a number of websites had picked up on the press story and had posted online articles. Samantha had googled herself in the past and had always been pleased with the links that appeared to various publications she'd been quoted in, all of which demonstrated her professionalism and expertise. This time, all that appeared were numerous links to her exposé of her client.

A reputation can be ruined in one fell swoop. Having gone from being a successful, professional and highly respected individual, Samantha found herself returning home after her holiday unemployed and with her career in tatters. There's a saying that many of you will be familiar with which is 'today's news will be tomorrow's chip paper', but thanks to the internet, paper print is the least of anyone's concerns these days. Online links, which are inherently difficult to have removed, will be there for weeks, months and years after the event and will continue to tarnish reputations.

Remember that your actions, whether in a professional or social setting, can backfire in a heartbeat. A moment of indiscretion or alcohol-fuelled fun, can be captured on a mobile phone camera as a still or video and then be posted online for the world to see without you knowing. If you are able to recover from it then you're fortunate; it can, however, be permanently damaging and have a greater knock-on effect than you could ever have imagined.

Understanding personality preferences

People are different. Some are gregarious and engaging while others are shy and retiring; some are organised and disciplined and others love spontaneity and going with the flow. No two people are the same.

This is important to recognise and understand when trying to build rapport – what works for some people simply isn't going to work with others, so you will have to modify and adapt your approach. It is helpful, therefore, if you understand some of those differences in personality type.

There are various type theories, but one of the most influential was that proposed by the Swiss psychiatrist and psychotherapist Carl Jung. It was this theory of personality type that was adapted and developed by two American women, Katherine Cook Briggs and her daughter Isabel Briggs Myers. They wanted to make Jung's theories more understandable and useful in everyday life and so the Myers–Briggs Type Indicator was developed.

According to Jung's hypothesis, when your mind is active, you are involved in one of two mental activities – perceiving (taking in information) or judging (organising that information and coming to conclusions as a consequence). Further to this, Jung suggested that there are opposite ways to perceive information and judge, or come to conclusions, which are:

Perceiving → Sensing or Intuition

Judging → Thinking or Feeling

Everyone uses all of these different processes every day. Sometimes they are used in the external world of people, things and experiences and sometimes they are used in the internal world of thoughts and reflections. Jung again divided these into two classifications – extroversion and introversion. Jung believed that everyone has a natural preference for using one kind of perceiving (sensing or intuition) and one kind of judging (thinking or feeling). He also believed that people preferred to operate in either the external or internal world. Some people have a strong preference for operating in one way, while others prefer the opposite. There is no right or wrong, or better or worse way, just different ways and this is what leads to differences in personality type.

The two Americans developed this theory and extended it, so that now the MBTI (Myers–Briggs Type Indicator) identifies the differences in personality type on four different dimensions:

- Where people prefer to focus their attention (extroversion or introversion)

- The way people prefer to take in information (sensing or intuition)

- The way people prefer to make decisions (thinking or feeling)

- How people orientate themselves to the external world – whether they primarily use a judging process or perceiving process (judging or perceiving)

This is not a book about personality preference, so if you would like to find out more then do explore further Jung's theory and the Myers–Briggs Type Indicator, but for now, what follows is a very brief summary of each of the preferences:

Extroversion: A tendency to focus on people and external events; directing energy and attention outwardly and deriving energy from interacting with people, external events and experiences.

Introversion: A tendency to focus on a personal inner world of ideas and experiences; directing energy and attention inwardly, deriving energy from internal thoughts, feelings and reflections.

Sensing: Taking in information through eyes, ears and other senses; recognising patterns and practical realities in the surrounding world.

Intuition: Taking in information by considering the big picture, focusing on relationships, concepts and connections; good at seeing new possibilities and different approaches.

Thinking: Considering logical consequences of a choice or action when making a decision; considering cause and effect rather than personalities; applying principles and rules to decisions.

Feeling: Considering what is important to themselves and others; empathetic and identifying with those involved in the decision so tend to decide based on values.

Judging: A tendency to live in a planned, orderly way with control and regulation; make decisions and move on; lead a structured and ordered life and stick to a plan or schedule.

Perceiving: A tendency to live in a flexible and unstructured way; love spontaneity and seek to experience life rather than understand it; prefer to be open and flexible rather than have a regimented schedule to follow.

There are sixteen possible combinations of these preferences and so there are sixteen different personality types, each with some typical characteristics, but remember these are preferences not definitions. They identify people's preferred type or modus operandi, but because these are only preferred ways of operating, that is not to say that individuals cannot also operate in a non-preferred way.

So, when trying to build rapport with people who you would like to include in your network, give some consideration to what their personality type may be, and what your own preferred way of operating is. If you have a preference for extroversion while your counterpart has a preference for introversion, then perhaps do not expect an immediate response to a question. While an extrovert will want to talk something through, an introvert will want to think about their response, reflecting carefully on the question, and thinking about all the possibilities before giving an answer. This can be very frustrating for the extrovert.

SUMMARY

You and your brand are key to building strong and effective networks. You need to be clear about what you stand for and how you want to represent yourself, keeping the message short, clear and succinct. How you look and sound is an extension of your brand and has a very significant impact, so be sure to adapt to your surroundings and where possible, match your counterpart's style and culture to build rapport quickly and effectively. Be conscious of differing personalities and adapt your approach accordingly.

5

Social Graces and Unwritten Rules

KEY POINTS

▶ Understanding the importance of good manners and the unwritten rules is essential in networking.

▶ Be aware of cultural nuances.

▶ Always remember to follow up after making a new contact.

▶ Your personal impact, your willingness to offer as well as receive and an ability to find common ground will all serve to enhance your networking ability and help to grow and develop your network.

Good social graces and being well mannered are not a luxury in networking, they are essential to achieve results and success. It's about being self-aware, respectful and sensitive to others. Social graces aren't simply about being polite and saying please and thank you, they are an attitude. We have already established that networking is about building relationships and respect is key to this. By showing respect to others and being thoughtful in our behaviour, we will in turn gain respect and that will open doors for us in both our work and social lives and people will remember us in a positive way.

How you interact with others is possibly the most important aspect of etiquette and is central to your ability to build rapport with people. At the heart of this lies your ability to create comfortable, easy and natural conversations that portray you in the best possible light and demonstrate your high levels of social intelligence. As we have seen, factors such as body language, speed of speech and such like are important during a conversation, but another key point is to try to understand more about the individual's beliefs, values, sense of identity and purpose in work and life. Noticing these things and acknowledging these points will ensure that you develop rapport and understanding at a much deeper level, which, in turn, will lead to a much more generative relationship.

Good social graces and etiquette should enable your own personality to shine through and encourage others to want to engage and build a relationship with you. When networking, you are likely to be interacting with a wide variety of people and it's essential that you maintain the professional image you have worked hard to achieve, regardless of the situation.

Keep an open mind. Often, the most interesting opportunities arise when you are least expecting them. If you aren't open to meeting new people, experiencing different things and taking yourself outside your comfort zone, you may well end up missing out on highly fulfilling opportunities either professionally or personally.

Consideration for others is the basis of good manners, so think before you speak and consider the following questions:

- Will this make people feel comfortable?

- How will this action affect others?

- How would I feel if I were in their shoes?

- Am I likely to offend anyone with what I'm about to say?

- Am I taking into account everyone I'm interacting with?

The best way to improve your social graces is through experience. You need to get up from behind your desk and meet people, whether that is at work, outside work or socially. It is much harder to build a good network by staying glued to your office chair.

Manners

'Manners maketh man' is the motto of New College, Oxford and Winchester College – both institutions founded by William of Wykeham in the late fourteenth century, and what is valid then remains true now. It may seem trite to say that good manners are important in relationship building but, remarkably, many business people neglect them. There are a number of things that can have considerable impact on how you are perceived by others and the impression that you leave them with.

RSVPs and punctuality

It is extraordinary how many people don't bother to reply to invitations. You have obviously been considered important enough to be asked to an event in the first place, so you should be courteous enough to tell the host whether you are able to attend or not. There is no excuse not to reply, particularly when a quick email will usually suffice. Not replying to an invitation is just bad form.

Many business people believe their absence from an event won't be noticed if they are too tired to attend at the end of a busy day. But if you replied that you were going to attend an event, not keeping that simple commitment can be perceived as a sign of your inability to keep your word on bigger issues – after all, if you can't commit to turning up at an event when you say you will, why should people trust your word in business? On occasion, there will of course be valid reasons as to why you are not able to attend a meeting or go to an event and these are completely acceptable. Do, however, be aware that if you regularly cancel meetings or say you're going to attend an event and subsequently don't turn up, you could be doing your reputation serious harm and you will end up being dropped from invitation lists.

If you do have to cancel then always remember to tell the person why you cannot attend. There are always good and valid excuses for calling off, even at the last minute, but remember to tell the hosts of the event that you're not going to be able to make it. After all, they will have made catering arrangements based on the numbers attending and they may be able to save some money if you give them enough notice that you cannot get there. Be honest and explain why, don't be tempted to make up excuses – the truth is always the best option because there is nothing worse than telling a lie and then being caught out:

CASE STUDY

Jackie had been having one of those days at work. Nothing seemed to have gone right, clients had been calling all day regarding problems they were having, two of her colleagues were off work ill and her boss was on holiday.

The last thing she needed was to be going to a black-tie dinner with a client that evening. She was tired, more than a little grumpy and didn't think she'd be good company for anyone anyway, so what was the point? She knew it was a bit rude to cancel at the last minute, but with the flu bug that was doing the rounds, which her two colleagues had been struck down with, she thought that would be the perfect excuse.

She called her client to say that she had unfortunately been taken unwell and was very sorry to be letting him down but she was feeling so awful that all she wanted to do was go home and go to bed. He was remarkably understanding and seemed genuinely concerned that she was feeling ill and agreed that going home was definitely the best option in the circumstances.

Feeling quite pleased with herself, Jackie breathed a sigh of relief at the thought of not having to endure an evening of schmoozing at a business dinner and was further heartened by seeing her best friend's name flash up on her mobile. On hearing that Jackie was suddenly free that night, her friend suggested that they meet up after work for a drink.

After a couple of drinks, they decided to go for dinner. Sitting in the restaurant, mid-way through the main course, Jackie was horrified to spot the boss of the client with whom she was meant to be at the business dinner a couple of tables away. She was just wondering if she could manage to beat a hasty retreat without being noticed when he looked over, saw her and waved. Horror of horrors, he then stood up and walked over to their table with a beaming smile. 'Hi Jackie, how are you? Nice to see you. I thought you would have been at the dinner event with Nick tonight, I'm sure he said he'd invited you and that you were going.' For once in her life, Jackie had no words to say – she was completely mortified.

Had Jackie just been honest with her client and explained that she had had a horrendous day at work and asked if there might be anyone else he could think of who might attend in her place, she could have avoided considerable embarrassment and damage to her reputation. Better still, she should never have pulled out of attending in the first place. We all have moments when we're not in the best frame of mind to do something, but in the interests of maintaining our professionalism, we put those moments aside and do the right thing. You run the risk of undermining your integrity and honesty in business, and at great risk to your long-term reputation. Funnily enough, it often turns out that going to something we didn't really want to can turn out to uncover the best opportunities so don't make the same mistake that Jackie did or you could find yourself in very hot water.

Punctuality is also extremely important. Turning up late to meet someone or to an event can give the impression of a laissez-faire attitude and even be perceived by some as a lack of interest and a lack of respect for other people's time. It can also be embarrassing to arrive late at an event and end up making a spectacle of yourself by walking across an entire room to the only empty seat. There will always be occasions where we are late through no fault of our own, in which case make sure that you send a message or call to warn them and apologise that you will be late, but try not to make a habit of it.

Handshakes

Think for a moment about when someone shakes your hand; it's not something that most of us tend to think about in a pre-meditated way. It can, however, have a big impact on the opinion the recipient has of you. Was it a limp 'wet fish' or a heavy 'bone crusher'? Or was it firm and genuine? A limp handshake can imply that you're not really particularly interested in meeting the person, or that you are lacking confidence. In contrast, the bone crusher may portray you as a controlling and dominant person who places themselves above you in terms of hierarchy.

It's interesting to consider how handshakes can also differ depending if you are male or female. Some men tend to make the assumption that when shaking a woman's hand, you should be very gentle while others don't give it any consideration at all. Both are wrong. When you shake a woman's hand, you may exert slightly less pressure than you would with a man – but avoid the wet fish at all costs.

Your handshake should be firm but not aggressive – the grip should come from your fingers tightening rather than your thumb. The thumb should remain firm but not tight. The general rule for handshakes is that they should last two to five seconds. There is nothing worse than a handshake where neither party seems to be letting go so do not shake the person's hand more than two or three times. Remember too that an integral part of the handshake is to look the person in the eye and to smile. You want to present yourself as an open and friendly individual with whom people want to engage. It is the first form of physical contact that you will have with an unfamiliar person, so make sure it's not an experience that leaves them dreading the next time you have to shake hands.

Introducing others and remembering names

If you want to break down barriers, you need to make people feel valued and the best way to do this is to introduce people to one another whenever the opportunity arises. People will generally take their lead from you; if you build a reputation for being a Connector, the likelihood is far higher that they will do the same in return.

When you are in conversation with someone and another person subsequently joins you, it is obviously common courtesy to introduce them to one another. This can be something of a challenge if you've forgotten their name! If you have approached someone or someone has approached you who you recognise but can't remember their name, this can be equally challenging. Don't make the mistake of hiding that you've forgotten. Everyone forgets a name from time to time.

If it happens to you then you can simply say:

> *'I'm so sorry, I keep wanting to call you Rebecca, you remind me of my colleague Rebecca but I know that's not your name! Can you remind me again what it is please?'*

Or alternatively, you can say:

> *'I'm sure you don't remember me, I'm James Cooke.'*

The chances are very high that they will then reply giving their own name. Whatever you do, don't make a quip about your bad memory or how appalling you are with names – such seemingly innocuous comments will only serve to plant negative thoughts about you. Making the point that you have forgotten is an admission on your part and although it may feel awkward, it is far less awkward than trying to bluff your way through an uncomfortable conversation and being caught out.

A useful tip to help you remember someone's name is to use it two or three times during your conversation with them. People always like hearing their own name and it will not only help to embed it in your memory, both at the time and in the future, but, it will also help you to engage with them.

Opinions

It is essential that you do not appear to be too opinionated when you meet someone for the first time – it's far better to remain neutral thereby avoiding burning any bridges. A good example of this would be if you are an avid supporter of a specific political party and you decide to wax lyrical about their policies to someone you've just met. How do you know that they will share your views and political sway? By doing so, you run the risk of totally alienating yourself from that individual and who knows, they could have been the very person who could have introduced you to someone with whom you wanted to nurture a pivotal relationship:

CASE STUDY

Stephen worked in the residential care sector and felt very passionately about new proposed legislation that had been announced the week before. He had already made his thoughts apparent to his peers and, not being one to mince his words, they were left in little doubt as to his feelings about the matter.

Stephen had been with his current employer for five years and for some time had been considering a move. Being a keen networker and with his usual professional approach, he had already identified one particular organisation where he felt he would be able to move up the career ladder and hopefully into a more senior role.

An event was being held to discuss the impact that the new legislation would potentially have on those affected. Care sector professionals in the local area were invited and Stephen was looking forward to attending. His enthusiasm was fuelled further when he realised that the CEO of one of the companies he had identified as a potential employer was going to be there. He hoped he would be able to introduce himself and make a good impression.

Once he arrived at the event, Stephen recognised a few familiar faces and joined a group of five people who were already deep in debate about the proposed legislation. Without wanting to be rude and interrupt the flow of conversation, he quietly slipped between a couple of people, smiling and establishing eye contact with all the members of the group.

One individual in particular was talking eagerly about how fantastic he thought the new legislation would be and what a positive impact he thought it would have on the sector as a whole. What a fool, Stephen thought, he clearly hasn't thought through all of the implications it may have, and certainly hasn't done as much research about it as I have.

After a couple of minutes, having heard enough to make him hot under the collar, Stephen felt compelled to interrupt and share his thoughts. He didn't hold back on his opinions, and while he wasn't rude, he felt very strongly about the case he was presenting and was clearly convinced that he was right. A couple of others in the group were nodding in agreement with what he was saying, which encouraged him further.

After a couple of minutes, the event organiser announced that everyone should start taking their seats as they would be starting in less than five minutes. Adhering to his principle of introducing himself to everyone he met, Stephen shook hands with everyone in the group, telling them his name and the organisation he was with. To his horror, the 'fool' whose opinions he had just spent the last couple of minutes slating, turned out to be the CEO he had wanted to connect with. To say he received a somewhat muted response when he shook his hand was an understatement, the icy look he received spoke volumes.

Had Stephen held fire on his opinion rather than reacting in the heat of the moment, he may well have discovered the identity of the other members of the group, thereby being able to manage the situation better. While the CEO clearly didn't share his opinion about the proposed legislation, that's not to say that the organisation wouldn't have been able to offer him his next step on the career ladder. And who knows, the legislation may not have been passed anyway so he had severely damaged any opportunities that might otherwise have come his way.

If you find yourself in a situation like Stephen did, it's far better to remain neutral; you may find the following phrase useful delivered with a smile: 'Well, that's one issue we're not going to solve tonight,' or simply end the conversation with:

'I certainly understand your point of view'. Whatever you do though, don't add a 'but' to the end of the sentence, however tempting it may be.

Always remain tactful, professional and don't be overly opinionated, there is nothing more off-putting than someone who forces their opinions on others, especially when they've not met you before.

Common courtesies

There are some basic guidelines you can follow for conversations at any event:

- Remember to say please and thank you.

- Don't interrupt.

- If you're going to get another drink, offer to get one for whoever you're speaking to as well.

- Keep your opinions to yourself when you first meet someone; be neutral to avoid offending someone unnecessarily.

- Be discreet – don't divulge confidential or sensitive information.

- Make sure that you RSVP by the date stated on the invitation.

- If you cannot attend for whatever reason, let your host know in good time where possible.

- Arrive punctually.

- Dress appropriately – black tie means black tie, not a lounge suit and tie, a dinner suit or appropriate formal regional dress with a bow tie.

- Put your napkin on your knee, it's there for a reason.

- Don't drink to excess.

- Wait until everyone has been served before starting to eat.

- Don't speak with your mouth full.

- Put your knife and fork together once you've finished eating.

- Leave your mobile device in your jacket or handbag, ideally turned off but certainly on silent at least.

- Don't apply make-up at the table.

- Don't chat during speeches or when films are being shown.

Cultural nuances and networking

If you are going to be a great networker, you are going to have to be a great communicator. With this in mind, you must be conscious of the culture in which you are operating and endeavouring to build fruitful relationships, because culture profoundly influences the way people think, communicate and behave. Culture, like language and even dialect, varies enormously from one region to another. Ask any Frenchman or woman what they think Parisians are like and you will be left in no uncertain terms that they view them differently from their other countrymen and women.

If you are trying to establish new relationships in a foreign culture then you have to be aware of the local cultural nuances and differences and adapt your approach accordingly. So there are two things to consider when you are networking:

1. How can you use your existing network to understand cultural nuances effectively and therefore build great relationships?

2. How can you ensure that you don't make a cultural faux pas that undermines you and your personal brand?

If you are travelling to another country, or meeting with foreign contacts, the best thing you can do is see if any of your existing contacts have any experience of that country. If so, you can ask about some of the cultural nuances they might have encountered.

The greatest risk that occurs is that you make assumptions about what is and what isn't a cultural norm, and such assumptions can often be flawed. One example is expecting that the saying 'When in Rome, do as the Romans do' always applies. As a practical rule of thumb, it is fair to think that business interactions should favour the cultural norms of the country and social environment in which that interaction is taking place, but that isn't always the case. It is, of course, always important to be respectful of the cultural norms of your counterparties, so the key thing is to do as much research as you can beforehand.

CASE STUDY

Iain worked for a recruitment company, which worked very closely with an organisation that promoted inward investment in his country. Iain's business was well placed to recruit for organisations that wanted to build manufacturing plants or take advantage of tax breaks that encouraged the relocation of innovation and research facilities.

Iain's first interaction with a potential investor was a nerve-racking experience. He had been assigned a new Asian client and had been asked to make a presentation to the board, who were coming over on a trip to meet the local teams and to have discussions about building a new semi-conductor manufacturing plant. Iain was justifiably nervous as it was not only a big issue for his own business, but also for the organisation that had facilitated this meeting. The CEO had given him some strict instructions: 'Make sure you don't make any cultural mistakes as these people are very sensitive to such issues.'

Iain did his homework as best he could. He talked to people who had worked in Asia and researched as much as he could about the cultural nuances before the day of the big meeting, which wasn't long in coming.

The Asians had brought a large team across and they met in the reception area outside of the boardroom of the inward investment organisation. There was a clear hierarchy around the introductions, which Iain had discovered was an important aspect of the process. Business cards had been offered and exchanged – holding them at the sides with the name upwards. Again, Iain had researched the protocols and complied perfectly but then he made his big mistake. Having collected the six business cards, he put them in his pocket and walked into the boardroom for the meeting.

He could not understand why he was on the receiving end of some frowns from both his colleagues, and the Asians on the other side of the table. Then he realised his faux pas. He had hidden the business cards away in his pocket rather than keeping them on display as everyone else had done – a sign of disrespect, as the CEO subsequently told him. He was mortified.

Even seemingly simple things such as business card etiquette can go a long way to building great relationships. Iain was trying to be respectful of the visitors' customs; he had done as much research as he could and talked to people with more experience of Asian culture than he had, but he still slipped up. It is, of course, not always possible to be prepared for every eventuality beforehand, but you might be able to pick up on additional clues by paying close attention to the behaviour of others around you. Had Iain been more attentive during the course of the meeting and watched how others had lain out the business cards, he might have avoided his mistake – perhaps, confident that he had done his homework, he had become complacent during the actual meeting.

A sound piece of advice is to try to put yourself in the other person's shoes and think about some aspects of day-to-day business that might seem appropriate to you, but which may cause offence to others. In the UK, taboo subjects for conversation are sex, money and death – yet others may be more than happy to disclose the value of the house that they live in and how much they earn. Indeed in some cultures this could be a way in which people reinforce their place in a hierarchy.

Think about the things that make you uncomfortable, what you avoid or what makes you cringe – then try to think about these issues from the perspective of someone coming from another culture or country. Even to the extent that you have developed your own personal brand – your handshake, your perspective on what is an acceptable distance to keep with someone (the personal space dilemma) or even the extent to which you make eye contact. As discussed earlier, what may be acceptable or appropriate for you in your everyday behaviours may cause insult to someone else from a different cultural background.

Cultural nuances can be a minefield, so use your network to understand them better but also do as much research as you can before trying to build a network across cultural borders. Here are a few things to consider, although this is certainly not an exhaustive list:

Relationships versus rules: Relationship-based cultures, like Asia, tend to operate with a strong respect of authority and hierarchy while rules-based cultures, such as the US or Germany, are anchored in a respect for roles. Clearly there is overlap between the two cultures, but the differences have implications for some of the other points in this list.

Deference: This is particularly relevant in relationship-based cultures. Deference can be experienced in grammatical inflections, body language such as the depth of the bow in Asia or the business card protocols.

Use of humour: The use of humour can be a real hazard in any culture. Germans may wish to focus on the business issues while Americans may like to diffuse tension by telling a joke. In any case, what is funny in one country may not cause smiles in another, so use humour only when you are absolutely sure that it isn't going to offend. If in doubt, *don't* try to be funny!

Demonstrating emotions: In some cultures it is not uncommon to be highly demonstrative with an emotional response, such as in Latin America. Other nationalities prefer to hide how they feel – for example the Japanese and many other Asians aren't usually highly emotional. Of course, much of this is driven by personality, so it is not a hard and fast rule.

Concepts of honour: Being sensitive to how people are regarded in their own hierarchies is crucial as this aspect can be very important in certain cultures. British self-deprecation or mockery of colleagues would not be appropriate in Asia for example. Similarly some Latin American and Middle Eastern cultures are very sensitive to situations where self-respect is involved. Tread with care and spend time understanding just what is going on around you in these environments.

Courtesy and greetings: Courtesy and manners have a very important role to play in some cultures. Acknowledging this and ensuring that you are aware of how to manage this is key to success. Be aware of greetings protocols: eye contact and a firm handshake may be appropriate in the UK, but in China it is customary to nod or bow – if a hand is offered, it should come from the host.

Punctuality: Punctuality (or lack of it) can be used to demonstrate the hierarchy in some cultures such as Indonesia, while in other countries, including China and Japan, punctuality is expected of everyone.

Communication and interpretation: Hard, direct or confrontational language in one culture may not resonate with a culture that favours more passive, plain language. Nuances in vocabulary can be very significant, so try to be aware of these both in your own conversations, and when listening to others.

Personal space: While in the UK and northern Europe personal space is valued, in southern Europe and in Asia people tend to stand much closer together.

When you are operating in an unfamiliar culture, in order to be successful you will have to be cognisant of the prevailing cultural norms. It isn't always easy, but time spent discussing these with people in your network will not be time wasted and, if in doubt, always err on the side of caution, taking the lead from others who you are with.

Following up

As mentioned before, following up is one of the most important aspects of networking and is probably the most critical step in leveraging your return on investment. You've met someone and impressed them with your professionalism, manner and engagement and you have said that you will be in touch with them but then they don't hear from you. Nothing is more unprofessional and damaging to your reputation than not delivering what you have promised. It is not only rude but it can also cause untold damage to how people view you.

If the person was a potential client, they may simply forget about you, and you will have wasted an opportunity. If you'd offered to do something to help them, they will lose faith in you. If it was someone you would like to work for at some point in the future, they'll be unlikely to ever employ you. When we say we are going to do something, we need to follow through on that commitment. If we are unable to do so, we need to be prepared to make things right. Trust is a very fragile thing, it is very easily broken and incredibly difficult to regain. People who have integrity are the ones that we trust and want to build relationships with.

Post-event process

It's all too easy to collect lots of business cards that subsequently don't see the light of day again until the next time you wear the same suit or use the same handbag. There is, however, a process that we recommend you adhere to, which will ensure that your actions following on from an event are organised and timely. By following this process, you will be much more likely to be successful in converting people you meet from mere connections to part of a mutually beneficial relationship.

1. Go through the business cards you collected and if you haven't already done so, write a reminder on the back of each one as a memory jolt – this could be a note of where they are going on holiday, how many children they have or what hobbies they have.

2. Prioritise who you are going to get in touch with and why – qualify them and be as specific as you can (our app BizPrompt can assist you with this).

3. Draft a general email referring to the event you attended, which you can then customise to be relevant and personalised to each individual you met.

4. Wherever possible, identify a hook you can share that will be beneficial to them.

5. Suggest an action, i.e. meeting for a coffee or lunch.

6. Add them on LinkedIn and start following them on Twitter, if applicable; include a link to your own Twitter account or blog if you have them.

7. Offer to help them with something specific that was discussed during your conversation.

8. Create your subsequent follow-up plan, i.e. how often you want to keep in touch with them and diarise a reminder.

By working through the steps above, you will start to build good relationships for your network. Relationships don't develop in a period of days or weeks; the most meaningful and beneficial ones will build up over time, so be patient and consistent and you will reap the rewards in the medium to long-term. However, at the start, being timely is critical. The general rule is that you should follow up within forty-eight hours – you want to get in touch with people while you are still fresh in their minds rather than running the risk of them having to wrack their brain to try to remember who you are, which can make it more difficult to re-engage with them.

When you get in touch with them, it's vital to link back to something in the last conversation or written communication you had with them. It might be a particular topic you discussed, someone you know in common, the fact that they are a keen golfer and were going to play a course that they wanted to play for a long time, or even that they were going on holiday to France. By linking back, you are continuing to build upon the rapport that you started establishing and demonstrating your interest in them as an individual as well as your good listening skills.

Give the person a reason to want to stay connected with you – you want them to see you as a relevant, worthwhile and engaging contact who they would like to add to their network of contacts. Here is an example of a suitable email (although do remember not to always hide behind emails, sometimes a letter or a phone call would be more appropriate):

Dear Simon,

It was a pleasure to meet you at the Townsend networking event on Tuesday. It was a great morning and the speakers were very interesting. I hope you enjoyed your golf at Gleneagles on Wednesday? As I mentioned, I've played there a few times and it never fails to disappoint, I am sure you will have found the same.

I said that I would follow up with you to see when it would be suitable to meet for a coffee to continue our discussion about developing new markets. If you would like to suggest some dates and times that would suit you over the next week or so then we can hopefully find a convenient time to meet.

I've been giving some initial thought to new markets and found this article that I thought may be of interest to you [either attach a document or add a website link]. I will add you as a connection on LinkedIn following on from this email and will start following you on Twitter. Please feel free to do the same, my Twitter account is @.............

I look forward to hearing from you and if I can be of any help in the meantime then please let me know.

Best wishes,

Andrew

The email above includes everything that should be on your follow-up checklist:

- A reference to where and when you met

- A link back to something the person mentioned when you met – in this case golfing at Gleneagles

- Action – what you would like to happen next

- A hook – relevant, helpful and of interest bearing in mind what you discussed, in this case the attached document or website link

- Link to social media platforms

- An offer to help

Personal impact

We covered the importance of developing your own personal brand in Chapter 4, but it's important to emphasise the significance of this in terms of etiquette. Your personal brand is central to your ability to develop strong and influential networks therefore you should always bear the key points in mind during your interactions with others.

- **Engagement:** When someone is speaking to you, you should always give non-verbal acknowledgements that you are listening to them. It can be too easy sometimes to lose concentration and zone out, especially if there are lots of other things going on around you, or if you're rehearsing what you're going to say next while they are still speaking. Make sure that you concentrate on actively listening to what is being said.

- **Body language:** This plays a key role in how we communicate and engage with others, so it's vital that you are aware of how even the smallest nuances can detract from your conversation, no matter how engaging it is.

- **Eye contact:** As previously discussed, you will now be aware of how much this impacts on how you are perceived by others, but more importantly, if your gaze is wandering round the room, you will simply appear discourteous.

Reciprocity

As discussed earlier, effective networking is all about reciprocity, and that is particularly relevant in terms of social graces, as it's the polite thing to do. Luckily the feel good factor comes into play here. The vast majority of people like to be helpful and most of us recognise that if you give to others, people will generally speaking return the favour.

Having said that, don't make the mistake of setting high expectations in terms of what you get back. Your philosophy should be to be willing to help others without anticipating or expecting anything in return. When you genuinely want to help others and create positive outcomes for them, your generosity of spirit is very apparent to the other party, which leaves them feeling good and will help to ensure that they appreciate the value that you bring to the relationship.

When you start hearing phrases such as 'That was a really great introduction, which will definitely lead to more,' or 'That was such an interesting link you sent me, it really got me thinking,' or 'Thank you for remembering that, I really appreciate it,' then you know you have a strong understanding of the individual you have been helping.

As a result, the people who you have helped will start recommending you to others and will become your personal ambassadors. We all know the power of word-of-mouth recommendations and you will reap the benefits as people start to recognise you as a key Connector. A word of warning, however: ensure that you always follow up referrals you are given in a timely manner. Good referrals are like gold dust and you should treat them as such.

There are few things worse than someone introducing you to another person in their network and then you doing nothing. Respect the fact that when people introduce you, it directly reflects upon them as an individual, so don't do anything that will show them in a bad light. You must also always remember to thank someone for any introductions that they do for you. By doing so, you are demonstrating your appreciation and they will, in turn, be more likely to do so again in light of your gratitude.

Conversely, if you are recommending a service to someone or introducing someone, remember that this will reflect on you. Never make the mistake of recommending anyone unless you are confident in their ability to follow through. The reputation that you have worked so hard to establish can very easily be ruined by someone else's actions, so if you have misgivings about someone, don't recommend them.

Finding common ground/connections

Finding common ground and connections with people is a frequent fear faced by many during their networking activities but it's actually incredibly easy when you know how (see pages 73–74). By finding common ground early on in the conversation, you can build rapport much more quickly, which, as we have already established in Chapter 4, is how you will build long-lasting and meaningful relationships with your network of contacts.

When commonality is identified, people feel more drawn towards you and will be keener to engage with you. If you're a seasoned networker, identifying common connections should be relatively easy. As we will discuss in more depth in Chapter 7, the internet offers many useful resources to assist you in identifying who you know in common either before an event or afterwards. If it's afterwards, that can be something you mention in your follow-up as your hook.

The easiest way to identify commonality with someone is to ask the right questions:

- 'What's your connection to this event?' This can reveal common connections or an interest in a specific area.

- 'What led you to work in your sector?' This can be an incredibly revealing question. As we've discussed, people love talking about themselves and their answer should give you plenty of insight into who they are and what interests them.

- 'What do you enjoy most about your job?' This is the best question to identify what makes them tick and if you listen carefully to the answer, you can use it your advantage on numerous occasions as your relationship with them develops.

- 'What do you do in your spare time?' Be careful when asking this question; some people will view it as an invasion of their privacy, so use your own judgement to gauge whether or not if it will be well received. The answer can be a very powerful way of identifying commonality on a more personal level.

SUMMARY

Few will have cause to criticise someone who is polite and has great manners. The biblical quote 'Do to others as you would have them do to you' is a sound maxim to live by and particularly relevant to networking. Relationships take time to develop yet can be destroyed or undermined by poor behaviour. You are never 'off the clock' and the simplest of slips can be damaging so be conscious at all times of your behaviour and how that is likely to be perceived by others, particularly others who may be influential in your world. If you do make a faux pas such as calling someone the wrong name then make sure you always acknowledge it and apologise. We are all only human and everyone makes mistakes from time to time so it's not the end of the world as long as you deal with it in a professional manner. Finally, be aware of cultural nuances – these have the potential to trip you up and cause unintended offence, so use your network to understand these better and be aware of them in your interactions.

Networking Events

▶ Networking events are an important way to build and develop your network.

▶ Focus on which events to attend, target who you would like to meet, and do your homework in advance.

▶ Engage in conversations and be curious – it's important to be both interested and interesting so that you make a real impact with the people that you interact with.

There are a host of different reasons why people attend networking events and you will find that your aims will vary depending upon the type of event you are attending. It's essential to remember, however, that networking events should not be viewed as a hunting ground for sales leads or as a competition to see who can collect the most business cards.

For many, networking events are the perfect opportunity to grow a contact list, while for others the prospect of attending an event is downright terrifying. Meeting strangers in an unfamiliar environment isn't exactly natural, so it does require some of us to adopt a very specific mind-set, overcoming fear of rejection being the most frequent issue.

One of the most common complaints we have heard over the years about networking events is being virtually pinned up against a wall by someone trying to sell themselves to you. That can be anything from professional services to a new website or printing, or even a request for a job. This can be extremely off-putting for the person on the receiving end of the sales pitch, so remember: do not be pushy or you will run the risk of having people avoiding you like the plague at future events. Think about your own personal brand and how you need to adapt your approach to reflect this – you may want to come across as being quite forthright and straightforward, in which case taking an assertive approach is the right way to go. On the other hand, if you want to appear modest and understated you will need to take the opposite approach and allow people to come to you.

As we have said, networking is not about selling (although you are selling yourself). In time, once a relationship has been established and trust has been built, there may well be a resultant 'sale' for either party but this should never be your primary focus.

Selecting the right events

A key challenge with networking is identifying which will be the best events to attend. These days, with a plethora of events on offer from early morning breakfasts to lunches, dinners and evening drinks events, there is no lack of choice. It can be easy to make the mistake of not having thought through who you want to network with and which events are likely to produce the results you are looking for according to your networking plan. Time spent planning, coupled with a focused approach to events will pay dividends.

You should also give consideration to what times fit best with your work schedule and also at what times of the day you are at your brightest. If you're not a morning person then, wherever possible, try to avoid breakfast events. You want to present yourself in the best light and if you struggle to come to until mid-morning, you are unlikely to be able to maximise opportunities first thing in the day.

A simple Google search for networking events should provide you with a good basis to start your research. Simply searching for networking events followed by the town, city or industry sector you wish to target will also yield plenty of results. One beneficial website to look at is www.findnetworkingevents. com, which lists networking events by town or city, region and gender as well as business shows. When searching for events, ask yourself the following questions:

1. Who do I want to meet and why?

2. What times of day work best for me to fit in with my work schedule?

3. Do I want to attend events in my local geographical area or in an area I wish to target?

4. What budget have I allocated to attend events?

5. Do I want to attend industry-specific events?

6. Who else will be at the event?

You should be aware that some networking events are run by member-only organisations, which require you to pay a subscription. It is important to weigh up the benefits of these before signing up as you may find that you are tied to a contract to be a member for a minimum amount of time. Member-only networking organisations generally tend to be less orientated towards selling to one another and more based around learning from one another and building connections.

Before attending a networking event, it's important to focus on your objectives. It is particularly worthwhile spending some time to try to find out as much as possible about who will be attending. Some event hosts will share the attendee list prior to the event, which makes it much easier for you to pre-plan who you would like to speak to. If this isn't the case, on arrival, ask your hosts if you can have a look at the guest list or, alternatively, get in touch with the organisers before the event and ask if they would be able to send you a delegate list.

If there are specific people with whom you wish to connect at the event then ensure that you do your research prior to meeting them – an online search will usually provide you with ample information. By doing your research you will be much better equipped to approach them in a confident manner, provide an appropriate icebreaker and make yourself more memorable to them. A small investment in time prior to the event is more likely to result in impressing someone and quickly building rapport.

Doing as much preparation as you can before the event will help you to know what to expect, who is likely to be there, which of your networking goals may be met and how you can potentially help others who are attending the event.

Working a room

For many people, the thought of walking into a room full of strangers is their worst nightmare. Even the most confident of us can no doubt empathise with the situation – you are going to attend a networking event, on your own, and you have no idea who else will be there and whether or not you will know anyone. You feel nervous – what if no one speaks to you? What if you forget your elevator pitch? How should you approach someone? What can you talk about without running the risk of garbled conversation?

We have already discussed developing your elevator pitch in Chapter 4, so, making sure that you have honed this and are comfortable with it, is the first step in building your confidence. But what then?

Remember that you are attending events to meet new people and expand your network, so first off, it's essential that you leave those you meet with a lasting and positive impression. Key factors that should be foremost in your mind include:

- Smile and be approachable
- Have an open mind, be interesting and interested
- Be aware of potentially mutual benefits
- Be confident
- Listen
- Have an ample supply of business cards
- Ensure your body language mirrors the words you speak

With that in mind, working the room is exactly as it sounds, with the ultimate aim being to produce results by finding and meeting good contacts and opportunities. The bottom line is that you will be spending time interacting with attendees; talking to them, listening to them and asking and answering questions. Take your time with each person and make sure you leave them feeling that talking to you has been time well spent. One of the most important aspects to working a room effectively is to remember that less is more: it's far more beneficial to speak to a smaller number of people and build good-quality connections, rather than taking a scatter-gun approach and trying to speak to as many people as possible in a very short period of time.

So what are the key hints and tips?

1. Try to find someone who is on their own to start your networking – but don't get stuck with just them for the whole event.

2. On the other hand, don't feel you have to leave that person – you can operate as a tandem and both of you go and join another conversation or group.

3. If you do need to leave, be polite and excuse yourself – at networking events there is an expectation that everyone will work the room, so it isn't rude to move on to meet someone else.

4. Introduce your group to newcomers and engage with people in the room – if someone is hovering outside the set of people that you are talking to, invite them to join you and introduce everyone; they will be indebted to you.

5. Make sure you cover the whole room, don't get stuck in a corner or find yourself pinned to the wall. Do at least three circuits of the room without talking to anyone in particular – you may bump into someone very helpful to you on the way.

6. Use your host(s) to make introductions – they should know everyone in the room. If there is someone that you particularly want to meet, ask your host to introduce you to them and if you can't meet them there and then, make sure you follow up after the event.

If you are nervous about attending an event, we recommend that you arrive early. It can be much less intimidating to enter a room with fewer people in it rather than waiting until most people have arrived. By being one of the first to get there, you have much more opportunity to engage on a one-to-one basis with a few individuals before the hustle and bustle of the event starts. The chances are that you will also have a greater opportunity to make a good impression on someone before they are bombarded with business cards and introductions.

Mixing and mingling is key to your networking success. It can be too easy to gravitate towards people you already know, perhaps even colleagues or existing clients, but remember your objectives: you are there to make new connections. If someone you already know well approaches you then don't be afraid to politely explain to them that you have a specific goal in attending the event and therefore want to make sure that you meet new connections. If they are a true networker then they'll understand!

Conversations: getting into them . . . and out of them

The focus in the forefront of your mind at a networking event should always be ensuring that your conversation revolves around the person or people that you are speaking to – listening 60 per cent of the time and talking and engaging for the other 40 per cent. Making the topic of conversation about them is far smarter and considerably more strategic than talking about yourself the entire time.

If you are nervous about networking, look for someone else who is standing by themselves and initiate conversation with them. Your approach should be friendly and open; walk over to them, smile, introduce yourself by name followed by your company name and offer them a firm handshake. Remember to keep your right hand free as much as possible, if you have a glass in your hand you're immediately disconnecting with the person you're trying to engage with by having to fumble around, changing your glass to the other hand, and potentially offering an icy cold handshake.

If you can't see anyone on their own, try to avoid approaching two people who are deep in conversation, it can be much more challenging than interrupting a group conversation. When you approach a group, make eye contact with one or more of them while smiling and when there is an appropriate break in the conversation, say: 'Hello, my name is Jennifer Woods, may I join you?'

During your conversations, use open questions to demonstrate to people that you are interested in them. Starting questions with who, what, where, why and how should always result in more engagement and will quickly help to build rapport.

The more often that you initiate conversations, the better you will become at it, so, be the first to introduce yourself or say hello, even if you're feeling nervous. When you take an active rather than a passive role, your conversational skills will develop, you'll feel more confident and less afraid of rejection. Examples of the sorts of questions you might ask or statements you might make are:

'How do you know the hosts of this event?'

'Who do you know here today?'

'What brings you here today?'

Once you are part of a group conversation, you should have the chance to have a look around the room jointly to see if you recognise anyone. If you do, don't leave to go and meet that person immediately, but point them out, noting that 'I see Geraldine Jones is here – I must catch up with her later'. This gives you an easy out when you have finished your conversation with your new acquaintances – you can simply say that you must go and catch up with her, leaving politely.

There are a couple of topics that should be avoided at all costs when you meet someone for the first time, namely asking them if they've been here before and discussing the weather. While both may on the surface seem like reasonable icebreakers, neither are in any way likely to encourage anyone to engage with you. People are more likely to engage with you if you introduce something relevant and current to the conversation. Remember, great networkers always bring value to their network, whether that is insight, information, contacts or news so try to think along those lines. Make sure you have read the newspapers that day and check your device to get any updates if the event is being run later in the day. There will always be something interesting going on at home or abroad to talk about. If it is a business related event, give some thought to what is happening in that arena – have there been reports from regulators that might be important; have any large organisations announced note-worthy results or have there been changes in personnel anywhere? Board members and CEOs are frequently changing so make sure you do your homework about this so you have something to talk about.

While being up to date on current affairs is important to help you appear well-informed, you should be careful about delving into the realm of politics and expressing strong opinions (see pages 135–138). If the conversation steers towards political views, it is worthwhile trying to gauge where people's political opinions lie before launching into a diatribe of your own political beliefs. Similarly, expressing any strong or forthright opinion on a subject that might seem controversial is probably best avoided as you never know what other people's views are. Tact and diplomacy are great skills to have in these large group situations, but it's probably best to save your personal views and opinions for a one-to-one situation once you know your network better.

Once someone has shared information with you, remember to ask them another question about what they have just said. This demonstrates that you're paying attention and that you care about and are interested in what they're telling you. This is the most effective way of building up rapport quickly with someone and the attention you have paid to what they are saying will hopefully be reciprocated.

It's important to never be afraid to ask for clarification if you didn't understand something. Feigning comprehension could end up getting you into very deep water and is to be avoided at all times. It's far better to say 'I don't think I understood that last part. Did you mean ...?' rather than pretend you have understood and run the risk of making a fool of yourself into the bargain with your response.

When engaging with people at networking events, make sure that you don't end up speaking to the same person or group for too long. We mentioned earlier that less is more in terms of the number of people you meet; however, if you are speaking to someone you are getting on particularly well with and are enjoying the conversation, it can be very tempting to continue speaking to them for longer than is strictly necessary. If this has been the case then it's the ideal opportunity to follow up with them after the event.

If you're worried about offending someone by leaving them, a great way to move on is to say: 'I've really enjoyed talking to you and I'd like to pursue this conversation further, but there are some other people I need to speak to. May I please have your card so I can follow up with you?' Another suggestion to remove yourself from a conversation (particularly if it's one you're not finding very beneficial or interesting) is to politely excuse yourself and say you need to get another refreshment.

Finally, you should always greet and close the conversation in the same way. If you have shaken someone's hand when you first met them, then do the same when you're moving on to speak to someone else.

Being interesting and interested

We have already discussed the importance of engagement and building rapport by asking open questions but there are several other factors that can demonstrate your interest in the people you are speaking to. By listening to what the other person is saying, you will be able to identify commonality, which in turn increases engagement more quickly. Ignore this at your peril:

CASE STUDY

Paul had just started a new role with a much bigger company than he'd worked for previously and hadn't really had much experience of attending networking events. He was a fairly outgoing individual so wasn't unduly nervous about networking, but being relatively new to the company, he was anxious to create the right impression, both about himself and the organisation, to his peers as well as to his manager.

He prepared his networking plan and his goals for his first event and, having been given a list of the other delegates who were attending, he had identified the key people he wanted to meet. He was comfortable with his elevator pitch and had practised it with both a colleague and his manager so was feeling very positive about the preparation he had done.

He arrived at the event five minutes early, introduced himself to his hosts and collected his name badge. Upon going through to the room where the event was taking place, he noticed a person who was standing on his own and decided to approach him. He introduced himself and said which company he worked for and asked his name. He replied politely, telling Paul that his name was Duncan. Paul then asked what company he worked for; three minutes later he was somewhat shell-shocked by the fact that Duncan was still explaining the history and track record of his organisation and his role within it.

When he eventually stopped talking, Duncan asked Paul if he'd been at one of these events in the past. Before Paul even had the chance to reply, Duncan once again took over the conversation and proceeded to give him a run-down of the many times he'd attended these events and all of the super contacts he'd met as a result.

Duncan's next question was what Paul did at his company, and, before Paul had time to utter more than two short sentences from his elevator pitch, during which Duncan had spent the whole time looking over his shoulder, not once glancing in Paul's direction, he interrupted again with a cursory 'Anyway, it was nice to meet you; I've just seen Angela arriving. She's very important so I must go and speak to her. See you later.'

Duncan is a classic example of someone who had neither self-awareness nor any idea how to engage with others. Duncan was neither interesting nor interested. Had Paul not been the resilient person that he was, he could easily have been discouraged about going to future events; however, he put the whole experience down to a sage lesson in how *not* to network and vowed that despite his relative inexperience in networking, he would never adopt Duncan's approach.

In order to be interesting and interested, adhere to the following simple guidelines:

- Ask open-ended questions

- Listen and ask relevant questions based upon what the person you're talking to has said

- Don't interrupt

- Maintain good eye contact

- Answer questions you are asked succinctly and follow them with a question

- Paraphrase answers to questions to check for understanding

- Plan your elevator pitch and use it

- Make yourself memorable for the right reasons

And please, avoid looking over the person's shoulder to see who else is around! There is nothing more disconcerting than talking to someone who is looking beyond you to see if there is someone more interesting to talk to. Give the person with you your full attention – there will be plenty of time to work the room once you have finished with that particular individual.

Curiosity

There is a fundamental difference between being curious in a positive and engaging way and being downright nosy. Some questions we have been asked at networking events fall into the latter bracket, which unfortunately is not only off-putting at the time but is also the enduring memory you are left with of that individual. Meeting someone at a networking event isn't about interrogation, nor is it about asking invasive personal questions. There is a very fine line to tread, so make sure you are aware of it and you do not overstep the mark.

Generally most people are happy to talk about themselves, so ask questions along those lines. Make sure that these are open questions, that you listen to the answers and where possible, ask a follow-up question. An example might be:

'So, where do you work?'

'I work at BFT plc.'

'BFT plc – they manufacture widgets don't they? How long have you been there?'

'Four years – and yes, they are a widget manufacturer.'

'How interesting – I used to supply a widget manufacturer with their raw materials. What do you do for them?'

You can see that the questioning above isn't simply a series of one question after another. Having done your research before coming to the event, you know a little about BFT plc so you can demonstrate that with your new acquaintance; if you have genuinely had the opportunity to work in that sector, make mention of it, so that you establish some common ground – it's the platform to build a new relationship.

It can also be a great icebreaker for when you next get in touch with them. People will really appreciate that you remembered they were in France in July and that they have three children or that they worked for BFT plc for four years.

CASE STUDY

Marion had been attending a course to further her professional development. This course was modular and took place over a total of ten days, split into three modules – two of three days each and the last over four days. Each module took place in the first week of the month over three successive months and was held at the same location – a lovely converted barn in the countryside where the learning environment was ideal.

The barn had a dining room attached to it and during the course delegates were served with wonderful food at lunchtime and during the breaks. Marion was quite an outgoing person with excellent manners, so she always took time to thank those who had prepared the food and who were clearing away the plates at the end of the meals. As the days wore on, so Marion engaged in deeper conversations with them, allowing her curiosity to take her wherever the conversation went – she was friendly and the staff were happy to open up to her.

Halfway through the final module, the Programme Director leading the course asked the delegates a question: 'We have now been here a total of eight days. I would like you to write down what you know about the two people that have been serving us food in the dining room and looking after us at break time please.'

For a moment, most of the twelve delegates had slightly bemused looks on their faces. To their shame, more than 50 per cent of the delegates admitted that they did not even know the names of the people working in the dining room – they had not allowed their curiosity to extend beyond their immediate circle of delegates. Marion on the other hand, had scribbled away furiously as she wrote down their names, the names of their children, what their children were doing, where they planned to go on holidays, how long they had been working at the barn, where they worked before they started here – the list was almost endless.

Marion was a genuinely curious person. She used that curiosity to learn – about people, things, places, work and whatever she came across. It was a quality that stood her in very good stead as her career progressed.

There will be times when you are very interested in things that people say and no doubt other times when you aren't. What is important to remember is that even if you're finding what they are saying somewhat tedious, the other person shouldn't be aware of it. If you can manage to subtly change the subject with your next question then you will know that you have truly mastered the techniques of skilled communication.

Making yourself memorable – what will they say when you leave?

We have already talked about many of the things that will make you memorable to others in previous chapters, including dressing in an appropriate manner at work and when attending networking events; listening to and being interested in what people are saying; and considering how others perceive you. Rightly or wrongly, people will form an opinion of you and it is obviously in your best interests to ensure they are left with long-lasting and positive memories of you.

It is human nature to make judgements and opinions about others that are very personal and often vary considerably from one individual to another. Think about the last person that you met at an event, what would they say about you? Would they remember that you had just been promoted into a new role that you were very enthusiastic and passionate about? Would they remember that you were very courteous and professional, ensuring that they were introduced to anyone new who joined in your conversation?

Whether they did or didn't depends very much on how you presented both yourself and the information. Was your parting comment that you would be in touch to arrange to meet for a coffee to continue the discussions you'd been having? Or that you would introduce them to a contact you have who could be really beneficial to the new market they were trying to break into? Did you meet at a dinner, at the beginning of which you were very professional and by the latter stages, you had consumed a little too much wine and were slurring your words while trying to press another business card into their hand having already given them one earlier? It's all too easy to end up being memorable for all the wrong reasons, so make sure that the lasting memory that someone has of you is a positive one, which will make them want to grow and develop their relationship with you.

CASE STUDY

Susan was delighted to have been invited along to a black-tie dinner by her manager at which they would be entertaining a number of key clients. She hadn't met all of them but had done her research and checked them all out online so felt pretty confident that she would have plenty to speak to each one about.

There was one organisation in particular whose account she would be managing. The previous incumbent had recently left and she was yet to meet the replacement, David. He had an impressive profile online, and had obviously been very successful in his career to date.

The guests all met at the pre-dinner drinks reception and the conversation flowed. Susan was pleased that she had done her research and had managed to engage with each client. She was getting on particularly well with David and felt comfortable that managing his account would continue to be as positive an experience as it had been with his predecessor.

Midway through dinner, with the wine flowing, the conversation around the table was interesting and everyone was getting on very well. David, however, seemed to have had more wine than water and was waxing lyrical about his successful career to date while seeming totally disinterested in anything that Susan said. Whenever she tried to speak he interrupted and he even had the audacity to tell her that she'd done 'pretty well for a woman', career-wise.

Although she was incandescent with rage inside, Susan managed not to react and ignored his chauvinistic comments, which were delivered in a slurred and demeaning tone. The event came to a close and reflecting on the evening on her way home, Susan thought what a pity it was that David had been so charming and engaging at the beginning of the evening yet had ended up being patronising, overly pleased with himself and his achievements, and downright rude.

David called her the next morning to say how lovely it had been to meet her and that he was looking forward to working with her. He had clearly forgotten about his conduct the night before. Susan remained unimpressed and had to work very hard to overcome David's rude and patronising behaviour from the event.

David was probably a very pleasant person and good at his job, but he made the fundamental error of having too much to drink and became rather obnoxious. Susan was left with a view of David that was of an unprofessional and not very pleasant individual. For the sake of her job and her own professional attitude, she would grin and bear it for as long as she was managing his account, but she would never forget the way he had behaved.

So be aware of the memories you leave with people you meet and make sure they are positive ones that will make that person want to continue to engage with you. As we've said before, a good reputation can take years to build and milliseconds to destroy.

SUMMARY

Networking events can seem close to purgatory for many but they can be extremely useful. Time spent planning and preparing will not be time wasted – in trying to discover who else is attending and might be useful to connect with, but also in preparing your own pitch. Remember that most people attending will be there for exactly the same reason as you; if you can help them make the most of their time then that in itself will be of value to you and them. Don't be afraid to leave conversations (politely) as it will give all of you the opportunity to go and meet someone else.

Social Media

KEY POINTS

▶ Having an online presence is an essential component in your networking mix.

▶ Do not rely solely on online networking; it should complement face-to-face networking activities not replace them.

▶ Make sure you actively engage with your online community.

▶ Choose the platforms you use carefully; taking a scatter gun approach will not only take up considerable time but will also dilute the effectiveness of your online activities.

In today's digital world there is no place to hide. From the social aspects of Facebook, Twitter, Instagram and Pinterest, to professional business networking platforms such as LinkedIn, more and more information is available about all of us than ever before. While Generations X and Y have grown up in the digital era, for some older generations many of these websites are still relatively new and, for some, completely unknown. But nowadays a considerable amount of networking is done online to supplement face-to-face interactions, so social media *has* to be a component in your networking mix, and which platforms you use is dependent on many factors. The caveat is that online networking should not be used instead of face-to-face networking. Used correctly, it is a highly valuable addition to your physical networking presence and is to be ignored at your peril.

As a general (but by no means exclusive) rule, social media channels such as Facebook, Twitter, Instagram and Pinterest tend to be widely used by the younger generation – in many cases with little thought being given to the impact this can have on their personal digital brand. We will look at some of the pitfalls later in this chapter.

LinkedIn is widely recognised as the leading business networking platform globally. With new members signing up every two seconds and an ever-increasing number of global users, the phenomenon of LinkedIn is growing exponentially and will likely continue to do so.

Social media checklist

Here is a checklist of some of the things you should be thinking about when considering your online presence and brand. We will explore some of these points in more detail throughout this chapter. Do be conscious that it is tempting to try to do all of this on as many channels as you can but, as with the challenges of connecting with your network physically, with the right frequency and using the right medium, you may be creating a rod for your back if you try to do too much too soon. You would be well advised to start with one channel and do it really well before you think about doing the same thing in multiple channels.

- Select which platforms are most relevant to you.

- Ask yourself why you have chosen the ones you have and justify your participation in each.

- Allocate enough time to participate in and manage each one effectively.

- Check your privacy settings.

- Create a content management plan – think about the type of information you want to share on the social media platforms you use. For example, if there are specific changes to legislation within your specific industry sector then plan your social media posts once these have been announced. Other examples here could include sharing timely posts about industry-specific conferences and exhibitions. Use a yearly planner to schedule in key dates and share your posts when most applicable.

- Decide upon your tone of voice in the messages you post across all channels. Make sure that the language you use is professional and appropriate to your position.

- Avoid the use of industry-specific jargon or acronyms unless they are relevant to and will be understood by your audience.

- Find your target audience and see what they are talking about.

- Engage with your target audience and share relevant content.

- Participate in online conversations.

- Identify how you will measure your return on investment.

- Maintain your network of contacts on each platform.

- Set up Google Alerts to be informed when your name is mentioned online.

Choosing the channels that will work best for you

There are an abundance of social media channels available, as mentioned earlier – other notable platforms include Google Plus+, Tumblr, VK, Flickr and Vine. Add to that blogs and internet forums and it's therefore hardly surprising that many people shy away from using social media platforms – the amount of choice can feel overwhelming, particularly when they don't know which ones will be of most benefit to them from a networking perspective.

For our purposes, we will be concentrating on the three biggest online networking sites – Facebook, Twitter and LinkedIn. As can be seen from the table below, there is still a considerable gulf between Facebook and the next most popular, Twitter and LinkedIn yet for business, LinkedIn remains the pre-eminent and most popular channel.

Platform	Number of unique monthly visitors
Facebook	900,000,000
Twitter	310,000,000
LinkedIn	255,000,000

Source: eBizMBA Rank July 2015

LinkedIn

LinkedIn is the most widely used online networking site for business professionals. These days it is rare to find anyone who doesn't have a LinkedIn profile and it is often the top link to appear when someone searches online for you by name. Profiles typically detail current employment details as well as past roles along with your key skills, interests, contacts and more, depending how much detail the member has included. Members can join groups, participate in group discussions, post status updates and write blog-like posts, to name but a few of its numerous functions.

There are many uses of LinkedIn – it is the best online tool currently available to build your network of contacts and it is increasingly used by employers and recruiters to identify and shortlist potential candidates for jobs.

Twitter

Twitter is an incredibly useful tool to engage with a wide-reaching, global audience as well as being a fantastic resource for information. The topics that you can read about are defined by the user depending upon who they follow. It is well worthwhile using Twitter to be aware of news and business updates that you can share with your network – remember you should always be trying to create value for the people in your network.

Facebook

Predominantly an online networking site for individuals, Facebook is seen as the personal equivalent of LinkedIn. Users have more control over their profiles and what is visible to whom than on LinkedIn. A considerable number of businesses have a presence on Facebook via Company Pages and use them to engage with their customers by promoting and sharing information as well as running competitions and more. With more than three times as many users as LinkedIn, it shouldn't be dismissed as a networking tool, but be clear about your privacy settings.

Blogs

Many companies have blogs on their websites and a very large number of individuals blog in their own right, rather than under the auspices of their organisations. Indeed, some people have made a career out of blogging. Blogs are in the public domain and viewable by any internet user. They are predominantly used to promote news, expertise, opinion, stories and information and for those who blog personally from a business perspective, to demonstrate their knowledge and underpin their expertise.

By blogging regularly, you can easily build a reputation as being an expert in your field, which in turn can encourage discussion and interaction with your audience, whether they are colleagues, clients or prospects. Your blog posts can serve to strengthen relationships with your own network.

Forums

There are a multitude of online forums where discussions take place, people can ask questions and post replies. In a similar way to participating in discussions on LinkedIn, forums are an excellent way of demonstrating your knowledge and expertise while building your online persona.

The number of channels is almost endless – there are new niche platforms being launched on a daily basis, some exclusive to online networking within specific industry sectors such as OilPro for oil and gas professionals. To be active on too many is a recipe for disaster, you'll spread yourself too thin, although deciding which ones are most beneficial to you will, to a certain degree, be down to trial and error.

As we have said earlier, start small and grow from a well-established base. It is easier to replicate a successful formula on a few channels than try to do too much (potentially badly) on a large number of sites. Time spent planning is unlikely to be time wasted, both in terms of your channel strategy as well as your content strategy. You will need to develop a social media personality and voice that is congruent with your 'live' personal brand and this will require some thought.

In order to gain maximum benefit, you will need to promote the platforms you are active on to your network. You can add links on your email signature and on your business cards and on your profile on your company website, if you have one.

Measuring your return on investment

It is extremely difficult to effectively measure the return on investment for your social media channels and, as with any matrix, you will need to choose some key metrics for each platform to analyse the impact it is having. Examples of such measures are as follows:

LinkedIn

- Number of connections
- Number of likes and comments on status updates and posts
- Number of interactions on discussions you post
- Number of face-to-face meetings that take place with your connections

Twitter

- Number of followers
- Quality and relevance of followers
- Engagement with followers
- Number of retweets and favourited tweets you post
- Visits to the website you list on your profile

Most channels provide insights for your account that can be hugely beneficial in analysing the effectiveness of your activities, and which will provide guidance in terms of what is working well and what isn't.

Purpose and pitfalls

The benefits of using social media effectively are numerous; however, there is one word which must be foremost in your mind and that is content. In order to engage with your audience, you need to be posting content that is relevant, inclusive, interesting and attention-grabbing. Don't forget that it can also help with your Google search rankings, making you more visible on a global basis – potential clients will be more easily able to find you and your network of contacts will be easier to build. You will be able to publicise your skill set, experience, knowledge and expertise to an audience that a few years ago would have been impossible to reach.

Managed correctly, social media can be a fantastic business development tool. It can help you to reach out to new clients and is a great way of being able to research people you wish to connect with before you meet them face-to-face.

To make the most of it, you need to engage with your network on the content that they post. When was the last time you commented on a post or status that one of your LinkedIn connections shared? Do you simply retweet or do you actually get involved in conversations on Twitter? If the answer to either of these questions is negative, then you need to build upon your interaction. It's not enough to simply be a passive social media user when it comes to networking; you need to allocate sufficient time to manage your platforms effectively.

There are various online tools that will help with managing content that you post, and one of these is scheduling. Social media experts tend to fall into two camps with regard to scheduling posts: many feel that this is sacrilege and should be avoided at all costs, while others appreciate the benefits it can bring, providing of course that it doesn't replace inter-action with your audience.

In our opinion, the use of these tools can be helpful in terms of allocating time to your social media activities, with the caveat that you must remain engaged with your followers and connections. Identifying links that you want to share can be a time-consuming process; however, Google Alerts can be a very useful tool to assist you. Set up alerts that will enable you to identify relevant links within your industry sector and areas of expertise or information that could be of value to your network. You can then schedule the posting of these links across your social media platforms at times of the day and week when your network will be most likely to see them.

We cannot emphasise enough that this doesn't negate the need for you to engage with your audiences. Be aware of when your posts are scheduled to go out and keep an eye on any interactions that you should be participating in and commenting on. Be smart about it; if you're doing it well, your audience shouldn't be aware that your posts have been scheduled in advance.

Managing your social media presence

Effectively managing your social media presence will take considerable time and effort. You will need to put time aside to think about what platforms will be most beneficial to you, what content you will share, how often you are going to post as well as how much information you want to be visible, quite apart from also putting time aside to create content.

Quantifying the return on your investment of time can be difficult to gauge as we have already said. Combine that with the fact that many of us have little enough time to spare in our working lives as it is and we have a challenge to overcome. Managing your social media presence could easily become a full-time job in itself.

As with face-to-face networking, many people make the mistake of thinking that social media networking success is all about the number of connections or followers they have, but this is totally wrong. It's far better to have a smaller number of high quality connections and followers rather than high numbers of irrelevant ones. The adage, less is more, definitely comes into play with social media.

Remember that once you start, you can't stop. You need to post at regular intervals and the tone of them needs to be consistent across all channels. Your online voice needs to mirror you as an individual and the way that you interact when face-to-face with your network. We're not suggesting that you need to be posting on all platforms on a daily basis; find out what works best for you in terms of the time you have allocated to online networking and find the frequency that works best for you.

It's important to bear in mind that many potential employers and recruiters will now check LinkedIn, Twitter, Facebook and other platforms at some stage during the recruitment process, often before you even know you are being considered for a job. As we've discussed previously, consistency is key, and it's no different for your social media channels. There's no point in having a very professional LinkedIn profile when people can see your Facebook posts and photos of what you were up to on Friday night!

If you're not sure how the privacy settings work for any platform, then visit the help section for each one and make sure that you have them set so that only the information you want to share is in the public domain.

CASE STUDY

Joe was the founder of a successful company that was a reseller of printers. The company had been given the opportunity to supply three high-end printers for a client it had been trying to engage with for three years and Joe was very excited about the opportunity. He rallied his team together and they were all putting in considerable effort and working extra hours to ensure that they had the best chance of winning the business.

As an avid LinkedIn user, Joe frequently participated in group discussions and had a particularly strong political opinion. In one such group, he noticed a discussion about the forthcoming general election, which had a number of comments from a variety of group members. Given his interest in politics, he was intrigued by the discussion and started reading through the comments. By the time he reached the end of the thread, he felt compelled to participate. Being of a particular political bent and feeling passionately about what had been said by others about the party he supported, he decided to add his own opinion.

What followed his impassioned comments was a barrage of further comments from others, some of which, from his perspective, were unjustified and misinformed. Feeling somewhat disgruntled by what he felt was ignorance on their part, he added further fuel to the fire by adding yet more comments, which resulted in yet more heated online debates.

Three days before they were due to pitch to the new client, Joe received a call from the managing director saying that they'd decided to cancel the meeting. Somewhat surprised and very disappointed, Joe asked why. It was, said the managing director, due to one of his staff having flagged to him the discussion that had been taking place on LinkedIn. He told Joe in no uncertain terms that he didn't share his political persuasion and felt that his comments had been unprofessional in the extreme. For that reason they had decided to withdraw the invitation to pitch and were now seeking an alternative supplier.

Had Joe stopped to think before posting his comments in the heat of the moment, and recognised that by doing so in an online forum they would be visible to potential clients, he would have probably thought twice about doing so. As it was, his lack of forethought resulted in him losing a potential client, a life lesson learnt and an action never to be repeated. As we discussed in Chapter 5, be tactful and don't force your opinions on others or you could end up alienating yourself from your network. This applies online, as much as it does face-to-face, perhaps more so.

Your digital brand and reputation

Increasingly, we hear stories about the media having picked up on something via someone's profile or account on a social media platform. While most of us generally don't have to worry too much about the media hounding us, we should always be aware of who might be looking at us online. A potential employer? Someone who is going to be at a net-working event you're attending? Someone who is keen to add you to their network due to your expertise and knowledge? A potential client? The list is endless, so it's essential that you bear this in mind when sharing that photo from the weekend when you were out with your friends dressed up as a chicken. Who will actually see it? If you are concerned about who can see your profile then adjust your privacy setting accordingly.

So what does your online persona say about you? Is it an accurate reflection of the person you really are? If you are going to develop an online presence on social media channels then it is important to do it well. Here is a checklist for the most popular channels:

LinkedIn

- Is your profile complete and up-to-date?

- Do you have a professional photo?

- Have you completed your summary section?

- Have you joined relevant groups?

- Have you claimed your name URL?

- Have you selected the information that you want to be visible to the public?

- Are your contact details up-to-date?

- Do you want people to know when you've updated your profile?

- Do you want people to know when you've viewed their profile?

- How many recommendations do you have?

- Have you added your Twitter account if you have one?

- When did you last write a status update?

- When did you last share a post?

- How pro-active are you in groups you're a member of?

- What company pages and influencers are you following?

- Are they relevant to what you do?

- Have you added your skills?

Twitter
- Is your profile complete and up-to-date?

- Do you have a professional photo?

Facebook
- Have you checked how your profile looks to other people including the public?

- Are your posts only visible to your friends or are they public?

- Have you decided to be visible or hidden to search engines?

- Are your other privacy settings set up how you want them to be including your photos?

Using LinkedIn effectively

As LinkedIn is the most effective online networking tool, we are going to focus mostly on this. There are several ways that you can best use LinkedIn to build your network. Status updates and posts are a great way of sharing information and you can choose whether to make these public or just visible to your connections. Your profile should be up-to-date and clearly define who you are, what you do, where your skills lie as well as your experience. It's not enough to simply have a list of past employers with no description of your job role, nor to have a blank summary section, so make sure your profile is as complete as it can be. This investment in time will pay dividends in the longer-term, most especially when building your network. Who knows, it may also deliver that dream job that you've been wanting to secure.

It is worth noting that LinkedIn is as relevant for students as it is for those of you who are in full-time employment. As soon as you leave school, you should create a LinkedIn profile. Add your parents' friends who have watched you grow up and ask them to write recommendations for you. If you want to gain work experience during holidays or are trying to secure a work placement as part of your course, having a presence on LinkedIn along with recommendations from people who know you will be very helpful.

Summary

Your summary is your personal elevator pitch. It should not be written in the third person as if someone else has written it, and it should reflect your personality. Ask yourself the following questions:

- What do I do?

- What am I passionate about in business?

- What do I enjoy most about my job?

- What things do I do best in my job?

- Is there anything else that I do which is relevant to my job role?

- What do I want people to think once they have read my summary?

Ask someone who knows you well to read it over and add anything that they think you've missed. Don't be shy, it's your opportunity to shine; just make sure you're not singing your own praises too much! Use key words that will help you to be identified in online searches.

You can also add documents, presentations and links to your summary section. Do ensure that you check for sensitive information in any documents before you post them as they will be visible to your connections, or to the public, depending upon the settings you have selected. Avoid the use of jargon unnecessarily unless, of course, it will demonstrate your knowledge and expertise in a particular area or industry sector, which will help to build credibility.

Photo

Your profile photograph should be a clear head and shoulders shot of you and you alone, in business attire. The purpose of your profile picture is to help people to recognise you when they meet you and people are more likely to engage with someone who has a profile picture rather than someone who doesn't.

CASE STUDY

Caroline was delighted, she'd been working hard on building her LinkedIn connections and had recently exceeded 500. Her profile was up-to-date and having rewritten her summary, she felt it was an accurate reflection of her experience, skills and personality.

Having reflected on her photo, which was a portrait she'd had taken at work, she decided that it wasn't a particularly good shot and decided to change it. Having browsed through numerous photos, she had chosen a full-length one of her at a business dinner. She uploaded it and then decided that it was a perhaps a little over the top to have a picture in a sequinned dress, so cropped it to display only her head and shoulders. Pleased with the resulting picture, she now felt happy that her profile not only read well but she also looked good. Job done.

What she hadn't bargained for was a message from an old colleague asking if she was wearing any clothes in her profile picture. What she had failed to notice was that her dress was strapless and it did indeed look as if she was wearing no clothes in the photo. Suitably chastened, she hastily changed it back to the original shot before anyone else questioned her professionalism.

So, while you may love paintballing, having a profile picture of you holding a gun dressed in camouflage gear may not be quite the image you wish to portray to the world. Equally, while we have no doubt that you love your children or your pet rabbit very much, their inclusion in your profile picture is irrelevant and doesn't portray your professional image, so make sure it's you and only you if you want to create the right impression.

Experience

Your experience section should be complete for all the jobs you have had. You don't need to go into too much detail for jobs that were many years ago; give more information on your last three jobs or your last ten years of employment. Don't be afraid to say what your key achievements have been in your job roles but do make sure that you avoid company-specific acronyms and abbreviations that won't mean anything to people outside your organisation.

Remember that you can reorder your experience if you work with more than one company. Simply click and drag each position into the order you prefer. You can also edit your title summary to say whatever you wish to be viewable in the public domain. It may be a generic, informational type description or it may list the company or companies you work with or own. It is entirely at your own discretion but don't forget that this is what any LinkedIn member will see regardless of whether or not they are a connection.

Skills and endorsements

LinkedIn will automatically allocate skills to your profile based on the key words you have used in your summary and your experience sections but you can also add your own. Be honest about the skills that you have, there's no point in embellishing them to make yourself look better because the chances are that you'll be caught out at some point.

Endorsements have been a controversial topic on LinkedIn since they launched. Many people feel that they aren't a true reflection, given that LinkedIn prompts you to endorse someone for a specific skill when you view their profile. You are not compelled to endorse your connections, it is entirely a matter of personal choice. Remember this when viewing other people's profiles too – the skills they are endorsed for may well have just been a click of a button by someone who doesn't truly know whether or not the person possesses this expertise.

Building your network of connections

How many times have you received a non-personalised connection request on LinkedIn from someone you've never heard of before? Or perhaps from someone who you have a few connections in common with but haven't actually met? It's very much a matter of personal choice as to who you accept and who you don't. In terms of managing your connections effectively, as we said in Chapter 5, it shouldn't just be a numbers game.

If you want to have relevant and useful connections on LinkedIn, we recommend that you only add people you actually know or have met. The only exceptions to this would be someone with whom you share a large number of connections, or alternatively someone with whom you would like to connect for a valid and relevant reason.

If you are adding someone as a connection then make sure that you personalise the connection request and explain why you are adding them. One of the biggest complaints from LinkedIn members is receiving random connection requests from people you don't know and have never heard of. Consider these two examples:

> *Hi Tanya,*
>
> *It was a pleasure to meet you at the Biz Bonus event this week and in the true spirit of networking, I would like to add you to my LinkedIn connections in order that we can keep in touch.*
>
> *I look forward to catching up with you again soon.*
>
> *Best wishes,*
>
> *Rupert*

And:

Dear Chloe,

Tim recommended that I contact you due to our common interest in developing business in India and thought it would be mutually beneficial to discuss further.

I hope you will accept my connection request and I'd be delighted to meet up with you. I look forward to hearing from you.

Best wishes,

Donald

Each of these invitations makes the connection personal rather than the automated 'I'd like to add you to my professional network' statement. Making it personal is likely to have a far greater success rate and will reinforce the budding relationship.

Remember that the character limit for personalised connection requests is 300 characters, so be succinct and make sure that the key points you wish to get across are clear.

Recommendations
The kudos attached to recommendations is as applicable online as it is to word of mouth. LinkedIn enables you to recommend individuals and for them to recommend you. Generally, if you recommend someone then you would assume that they will in return recommend you and, indeed, LinkedIn prompts them to do so.

If you are asking for a recommendation then make sure that, as with connection requests, you edit the standard email to personalise it. By doing so you can explain why you are asking for the recommendation and offer to do the same in return for them, assuming, of course, that you know them well enough and are confident in their skills and ability:

Dear Robert

I am in the process of building up recommendations on my profile from key clients with whom I have worked closely and wondered if you would be good enough to write one for me please? I will, of course, be happy to return the favour.

If you have any questions in the meantime or would like to discuss further then please don't hesitate to let me know.

Many thanks in advance and I look forward to hearing from you.

Best wishes,

Janet

Communicate

As we have discussed throughout this book, communication is key and communicating on LinkedIn is no different. In order to build our networks and become more visible, we need to be seen to be engaging with our audiences. Ensure that every status update you write on LinkedIn is written using the same tone and relevant to whoever will see it.

When you add a post, make it interesting, engaging and, wherever possible, add images and online links. Remember to use spellcheck and to check your grammar before posting it; there is nothing more amateurish than poor grammatical errors and typos.

Remember that posts and status updates are not solely for the purpose of self-promotion, although there will be occasions when this is applicable. Use your status updates and posts to underline your expertise and knowledge, which will in turn enhance your online presence. You can also tag people and companies in your updates and posts, which can increase engagement with individuals and organisations.

Participation

Being a member of and participating in relevant groups are great ways of further enhancing your online presence and demonstrating your expertise and knowledge. Always remember that you never know who will be reading your comments, so remain neutral and be careful not to write anything that could be misconstrued or misunderstood, thereby damaging your reputation.

Meet

We mentioned earlier in this chapter and in previous ones the importance of meeting people face-to-face to build upon and maintain your relationship with them. LinkedIn is not a resource to replace the all-important physical networking in a face-to-face environment; it is complementary to it. You must ensure that you get out there and meet your connections to enhance the relationships that you have with them. Be careful that you don't become a pest, however, and remember to give them a reason or offer some value to them in order to guarantee that they want to meet you.

Using Twitter effectively

Many of the things we have discussed regarding LinkedIn are just as applicable to Twitter, including engaging with your audience, posting value-added links that will benefit your followers, sharing content of interest to a wider user base and of course underpinning your knowledge and expertise.

One important factor to emphasise is that it is not enough to simply retweet. While doing so may be appreciated by the person who tweeted in the first place, clicking a button is not real engagement. By all means retweet relevant and interesting comments, but nothing is more powerful than creating your own content, asking questions of your followers and subsequent engagement with them.

Always be aware that whatever you tweet can be seen by anyone, not just people who follow you unless your tweets are protected. Always think before you tweet and be aware that if you make a derogatory or incorrect statement, it could have considerable repercussions in the future.

SUMMARY

▶ Developing a strong online profile is an important part of networking. There are many channels to choose from, so you will be well advised to 'start small' and grow from a well-established base, just as you should have done with your physical network.

▶ Your online brand should be congruent with your personal brand and you should use the online channels to extend your network and to bring value to your contacts and connections. Be conscious of the pitfalls and the reach of the internet – it is the window for the world to look at you and what you are up to.

▶ If you manage your online brand well this will really add value to you and your network, but do not forget that the physical aspects of networking should not be forgotten. Humans need physical interactions as a matter of course; it's an important part of developing long-lasting, meaningful relationships, so don't be tempted to hide behind a computer screen or hand-held device.

The BizPrompt App

If, in reading this book, you have taken our advice on how to build and maintain a network and you are ready to get going, the one area that is likely to prove tricky is that of reminding yourself to connect with those in your network. Listing your contacts, prioritising them and developing a plan is all very well and good, but wouldn't it be brilliant if there was something that could remind you to contact people?

This is why we came up with the idea of the BizPrompt app – a simple and straightforward reminder system for you.

The BizPrompt app takes into account the key principles of our networking techniques. To use it effectively, you simply have to do four things:

1. Create a list of the people in your network. Don't make the list too long: BizPrompt has plenty of capacity, but it is difficult to have meaningful contact with too many people. Remember why each person is in your network and the reason for connecting with them, and aim for Dunbar's number of around 150, or a maximum of 200, at least to start with.

2. Load your chosen contacts into the BizPrompt app – you can do so from your Outlook, Gmail or other email contact lists. It is very intuitive and simple – we didn't want to overcomplicate things.

3. Prioritise each of your contacts into your three categories: 1 if you want to connect with them monthly; 2 if you want to connect quarterly; and 3 if you want to connect with them twice a year. That is a rough guide, but you'll soon develop your own rhythm in your networking.

4. Let BizPrompt work for you – the app will remind you when to touch base with your contacts. Just remember to make the connection meaningful when you text, email or give them a call.

As you add and grow your network, you should constantly be evaluating who might drop out of the network – otherwise you will end up with a large and unwieldy database of contacts. So remember to adjust the contacts in the app accordingly.

It's no more complicated than that and using BizPrompt will enable you to manage and maintain your network in a simple and straightforward way. Available to download in all app stores, it will be your personal contact relationship management system and we're confident that you will soon be unable to remember how you networked effectively without it. Good luck!

In Conclusion

Networking should not feel like a burden. It will certainly feel more natural for some people than for others yet it is for everyone. If you haven't done much networking before now then the mere word may fill you with dread. But do it well and it can give you a great sense of achievement; it can help you realise your career ambitions and it will help you continue to learn new and exciting things. You never know, you might even end up enjoying it.

What we have attempted with this book is to provide you with some insights into both 'what to do' and 'how to do it'. Networking is relatively easy if you approach it in a systematic and structured way. Breaking down the process into simple steps is key. Once you have done this it will not seem to be quite as daunting. What's more, you will appreciate that you have a better network than you think.

Remember, networking has to be done with purpose. Always be clear about the reason for your activity – if you don't have a good reason, then you should not be doing it. A clear purpose is at the heart of good networking and that clarity of purpose will define the value of the activity for you. The systematic approach that we have espoused should make life easy and even enjoyable.

You can build a great network from a relatively modest start, so no matter how concerned you may feel about the current state of your network, don't worry. By following our guide, you can and will make the connections and meet the contacts that you need.

Be clear about your own brand and how you want to project it with people. Be consistent and always remember the guidelines about how to network – the social graces, unwritten rules and need to give as well as receive. As ever, practice makes perfect so the more you invest time in networking, so the greater and more fulfilling your networking will be. Use tools such as the BizPrompt app to support your networking activities, so that they don't feel like an effort.

Digital networking is very important but should supplement your real life activity, not replace it. There are a multitude of channels that you can use but avoid the temptation to participate in all of them. Remember, as humans, our brains have evolved to need genuine social interaction and human contact, which isn't available on Facebook and LinkedIn.

So good luck with your networking – we hope that you will find it as fulfilling as we have.

Acknowledgements

There have been many clients and colleagues who, over the years, have helped us learn to network better ourselves – sometimes through their own great practice and sometimes through their mistakes. Many of the lessons we have learned first-hand appear in the book as a result.

We would like to thank all of those people who have read draft text and given us great feedback along the way. It has all helped to shape the final manuscript and we are very grateful to everyone for giving so generously of their time.

To our publishers at Elliott & Thompson – a thousand thank yous! You have been enormously helpful throughout the whole process, even with such tight deadlines, and your advice and insights have made a real difference.

Thanks are also due to Chris and Iain – the brains behind the BizPrompt app. It's our belief that this technology will make networking so much simpler than before.

Finally, to our families: we could not have done this without your unfailing support and encouragement – thank you!

Bibliography

Dunbar, R. I. M., 'Neocortex size as a constraint on group size in primates', *Journal of Human Evolution* 20 (1993), 469–493

Gladwell, Malcolm, *The Tipping Point* (New York: Little, Brown, 2000)

Briggs Myers, Isabel; McCaulley, Mary H.; Quenk, Naomi L.; Hammer, Allen L., *MBTI Manual: A Guide to the Development and Use of the Myers–Briggs Type Indicator* (Palo Alto: Consulting Psychologists Press, 1998)

Hall, Edward T., *The Hidden Dimension* (New York: Anchor Books, 1988)

HBR Guide to Networking (Watertown: Harvard Business Review Press, 2014)

Hobsbawm, Julia, 'Fully connected: a look ahead to working and networking in 2020' (EY, March 2014)

Hooker, John, 'Cultural differences in business communication', Tepper School of Business, Carnegie Mellon University (December, 2008)

Hughes, Damian, *How to Change Absolutely Anything* (Harlow: Pearson Education Ltd, 2012)

Lieberman, Matthew D., *Social: Why Our Brains Are Wired to Connect* (Oxford: OUP, 2013)

Mehrabian, Albert, *Silent Messages: Implicit Communication of Emotions and Attitudes* (Boston: Wadsworth Publishing, 1972)

Newman, Martyn, *Emotional Capitalists: The New Leaders* (Chichester: John Wiley & Sons, 2008)

Peters, Steve, *The Chimp Paradox* (London: Vermilion, 2012)

Salacuse, Jeswald W., 'The top 10 ways that culture can affect international negotiations', *Ivey Business Journal* (March/April 2005)

Singleton, Adam, 'Why observing foreign culture can lead to business success' http://ezinearticles.com/?Why-Observing-Foreign-Culture-Can-Lead-To-Business-Success&id=617467 (22 June 2007)

Thorndike, Edward, 'A Constant Error in Psychological Ratings', *Journal of Applied Psychology* 4 (1920), 25

Wilson, Timothy, *Strangers to Ourselves: Discovering the Adaptive Unconscious* (Cambridge, MA: Harvard University Press, 2002)

Index